W9-AWS-922

SATAN
EXPOSED

Books by Larry Richards*

*This is a partial listing

SATAN EXPOSED

DEFEATING THE POWERS OF DARKNESS

LARRY RICHARDS

Chosen

a division of Baker Publishing Group
Minneapolis, Minnesota

© 2015 by Lawrence O. Richards

Published by Chosen Books
11400 Hampshire Avenue South
Bloomington, Minnesota 55438
www.chosenbooks.com

Chosen Books is a division of
Baker Publishing Group, Grand Rapids, Michigan

Printed in the United States of America

All rights reserved. No part of this publication may be reproduced, stored in a retrieval system, or transmitted in any form or by any means—for example, electronic, photocopy, recording—without the prior written permission of the publisher. The only exception is brief quotations in printed reviews.

Library of Congress Cataloging-in-Publication Data
Richards, Larry.
    Satan exposed : defeating the powers of darkness / Larry Richards.
        pages cm
    Includes index.
    Summary: "Exposing Satan's origin, strategies, and destiny through Scripture, Larry Richards reveals practical tools you can use to hinder the devil's schemes"—Provided by publisher.
        ISBN 978-0-8007-9586-3 (pbk. : alk. paper)
    1. Spiritual warfare--Biblical teaching. 2. Christian life. I. Title
BS680.S73R55 2015
235'.47—dc23   201501572

Unless otherwise indicated, Scripture taken from the HOLY BIBLE, NEW INTERNATIONAL VERSION®. Copyright © 1973, 1978, 1984 Biblica. Used by permission of Zondervan. All rights reserved.

Scripture quotations identified TLB are from *The Living Bible*, copyright © 1971. Used by permission of Tyndale House Publishers, Inc., Wheaton, Illinois 60189. All rights reserved.

Cover design by Kirk DouPonce, DogEared Design

15   16   17   18   19   20   21   7   6   5   4   3   2   1

In keeping with biblical principles of creation stewardship, Baker Publishing Group advocates the responsible use of our natural resources. As a member of the Green Press Initiative, our company uses recycled paper when possible. The text paper of this book is composed in part of post-consumer waste.

Contents

Contents

Foreword

The Bible portrays the powers of darkness as seeking to bring harm to humanity and to blind people—even people in the Church—to God's way of restoration and wholeness (see 2 Corinthians 4:4; 11:3). For those with eyes to see the spiritual battle, like Elisha's unnamed servant in 2 Kings 6, we can witness its effects on the evening news and in the hurting lives of people we care about.

In this book, Larry Richards helpfully applies the principles of spiritual warfare to the practical nitty-gritty of our lives. In the Bible, spiritual warfare applies, for example, to marriage. Division in our marriages can hinder our prayers (see 1 Peter 3:7), and other problems in marriage allow Satan's temptations (see 1 Corinthians 7:5). Spiritual warfare also applies to other relationships in the Body of Christ. One of Satan's strategies is to keep us from forgiving one another (see 2 Corinthians 2:10–11), and we should bless even those who curse us (see Luke 6:28).

Dr. Richards speaks of how Satan distorts God's good gifts, carrying on a strategy that Satan has been using since the Garden of Eden. Resisting the devil's schemes, then, means using God's gifts in the right ways, and this is an opportunity that confronts us every day. In fact, the context of the Bible's warning not to give ground to the devil (see Ephesians 4:27) is about how we should serve, bless and forgive others rather than mistreat them. In another context, resisting the devil has to do with resisting the world's selfish and hurtful values (see James 4:7).

The Bible suggests that the evil one is at work not only in the ways that are most conspicuous to us but also through the wider values of the world system, values that play on human lusts (see Ephesians 2:2–3; 1 John 5:19). No wonder God's armor in Ephesians 6:14–17 includes matters such as righteousness, truth and faith. Of course, the powers of darkness do have more overt means of operation, but too often we miss the ways that they work through the values around us to distort God's purposes for our lives. Satan tried to redefine Jesus' role as God's Son according to worldly models of power, but Jesus stood firm by following the model offered in Scripture (see Matthew 4:3–10).

Larry Richards offers an abundance of spiritual insights about family, church and community that reflect years of experience and observation. He also shares them in the sensitive and pastoral way of one who understands ordinary people and the issues that we struggle with. The book is full of grace and takes into account the different kinds of situations in which individuals find themselves.

This book addresses real-life issues that each of us faces, explained with real-life illustrations. It is enjoyable and easy to read, but challenges us with eminently practical ways that we can make a difference where God has placed each of us.

Craig Keener, professor of biblical studies,
Asbury Theological Seminary, Wilmore, Kentucky

Introduction

It seems strange when we consider it. God, the Creator and supreme power in the universe, is at war with one of His own creatures. This war, which originated in the spirit realm, has spilled over into our world, to impact our lives in many ways.

In this book we will not focus on how to defend ourselves from demonic oppression, or how to cast out evil spirits. I have discussed each in earlier books from Chosen: *The Full Armor of God* and *Spiritual Warfare Jesus' Way*. In this book we will expose strategies Satan has developed to corrupt relationships and institutions on a grander scale. We will examine tactics Satan uses to carry out these strategies. And we will discover how we can live, not as victims, but as God's warriors in what is essentially a struggle between good and evil.

In the process, we will discover how we can defeat the powers of darkness.

Raleigh, North Carolina

PART 1

UNDERSTANDING THE INVISIBLE WAR

1

The Hidden Background

By the time God fashioned the earth as a home for human beings, He was already at war with a host of spirit beings. In the Old Testament, spirit beings are typically referred to as *elohim*, a term that means, essentially, "supernatural beings," and refers to both good and evil angels, although *elohim* is often rendered "God" or "gods."

God had long ago created these spirit beings as angels. For an unknown expanse of time they served Him loyally. Then one of the most powerful of the angels, a cherub known as "Morning Star" and "Light Bearer," rebelled (see Isaiah 14; Ezekiel 28). Ezekiel describes this being as "the model of perfection" (Ezekiel 28:12) and "blameless in your ways from the day you were created till wickedness was found in you" (verse 15).

Isaiah reveals the burning passion that drove this fallen angel, whom we know as Satan. Isaiah describes Satan's intent in a series of "I will" affirmations:

You said in your heart, "I will ascend to heaven; I will raise my throne above the stars of God; I will sit enthroned on the mount of assembly, on the utmost heights of the sacred mountain. I will ascend above the tops of the clouds; I will make myself like the Most High."

Isaiah 14:13–14

In short, Satan determined to make himself supreme, and supplant God as ruler of the universe.

Satan was not alone in his attempt to replace God. A number of *elohim* joined his rebellion. But an even greater number of *elohim*, those whom we know today as angels, remained loyal to the Creator. That rebellion, launched long before Genesis 1, pitted Satan and his followers, today called demons, or evil spirits, against God and His angels. The result is war between God and Satan, between angels and demons.

The Opening Battle

Scripture gives us glimpses into the opening battle in the war. Jesus, speaking to disciples who were excited that demons were subject to them in Christ's name, told them: "I saw Satan fall like lightning from heaven" (Luke 10:18). His words echo those of Isaiah, who introduces Satan's proud "I will" statements by saying: "How you have fallen from heaven, O morning star, son of the dawn! You have been cast down to the earth" (Isaiah 14:12).

Ezekiel echoes the same theme: "This is what the Sovereign LORD says: . . . 'I drove you in disgrace from the mount of God, and I expelled you, O guardian cherub. . . . So I threw you to the earth'" (Ezekiel 28:12, 16–17).

Satan's pride and passion drove him to lead a rebellion against the Creator. But in the initial battle, Satan and his forces were decisively defeated. Satan was "expelled," fell "from heaven" and was "cast down to earth." This same initial battle is possibly described in Revelation 12:7–9, although set in the context of future events.

> And there was war in heaven. Michael and his angels fought against the dragon, and the dragon and his angels fought back. But he was not strong enough, and they lost their place in heaven. The great dragon was hurled down—that ancient serpent called the devil or Satan, who leads the whole world astray. He was hurled to the earth, and his angels with him.

The Bible offers only scattered images of the initial battle. Yet, the same images are found in Old Testament prophecies, in the words of Jesus and in the powerful scenes in Revelation. Satan rebelled. There was a struggle. Satan and his followers were expelled from God's realm. Satan and his angels were "hurled to the earth."

We do not know when this battle between angels and demons was fought. Clearly, though, it occurred before the events described in Genesis. In particular, the seven days creation account does not include *elohim*, yet both Satan and God's angels appear in Genesis' early chapters. Along with the timing of the battle, we learn something about its location. The creation of angels and their rebellion took place in a spirit universe, one the apostle Paul calls "the heavenly realms." Those realms run parallel to the material universe in which we live. And, as we open the Bible to its earliest chapters, we realize that the "war in heaven" has definitely spilled over into our physical realm.

Earth As a War Zone

The first two verses of Genesis state that God created the heavens and the earth, and describe the earth as "formless and empty," shrouded in a darkness that concealed the surging waters of "the deep." This is a very different picture of our planet from that found in the rest of Genesis 1, which describes God fashioning the earth we know today. The mystery deepens when we read in Isaiah 45:18 that when God founded the heavens and made the earth, "he did not create it to be empty, but formed it to be inhabited." The same Hebrew word describing the earth as "formless and empty" in Genesis 1:2 is used here in Isaiah.

In this the Bible suggests a fascinating possibility. That "formless and empty" earth described in Genesis 1:2 can hardly be viewed as a place "to be inhabited." Rather than a pleasant land, Genesis 1:2 seems to picture a war zone, a planet left in ruins in the aftermath of a titanic battle. Perhaps that battle, which Satan and his angles lost decisively, resulted in their being expelled from heaven and thrown violently to earth?

It is this picture of a ravaged planet that greets us when we first open our Bibles. But Scripture adds: "The Spirit of God was hovering over the waters" (Genesis 1:2). God was not finished with our earth, or with the enemy He had isolated here.

A Renewed Earth

The next verse shows God acting to redeem or refurbish His original creation. God said, "'Let there be light,' and there was light" (Genesis 1:3). He spoke again and again, separating the waters (see verses 6–8), causing dry ground to appear (see verse 9), filling the earth with vegetation (see verses 11–13), establishing a regular pattern with time and seasons marked by sun and moon (see verses 14–19), filling the waters and the land with living creatures (see verses 20–25), and then fashioning human beings in His own image and likeness (see verses 26–31).

There are several things that are important in the account of the creation—or more likely, the refashioning—of the material universe, and of earth in particular.

First, in Genesis 1 God introduces Himself to us. We meet Him in all those things He calls *good*, a term repeated seven times in this chapter. To God, separating light from darkness is good. To God, life on a planet designed to meet the needs of all living things is good. To God, a stable universe with day following night and season following season is good. To God, human beings shaped in His own image are "very good."

In this we meet a God who truly is like us. The things that seem good to Him are things we experience as good as well. The refurbished earth, not an earth that is formless, dark and empty, is where we feel at home. Satan and his evil spirits may delight in chaos, but we human beings need order, consistency, beauty and light.

Genesis 2 describes Adam's life in Eden, and further underlines ways that we and God are alike. In the Garden, Adam, like God, experienced beauty (see Genesis 2:9). Like God, Adam found fulfillment in meaningful work (see verse 15). And, through naming the animals and finding no one to whom he could relate, Adam, like God, sensed a need for someone in his own image to love and to be loved by (see verses 19–20). Then God acted to meet Adam's need for love

17

by creating Eve, a "suitable helper," a partner with whom he might share life here on earth.

In all this we learn that the God of Creation is a God of love, a God who, in creating us in His own likeness and image, invites us to experience a personal relationship with Him. Millenniums later we discover how deeply God loves us, when God the Son becomes man and sacrifices Himself for us. Genesis is just the beginning of the story. Yet even in this beginning we learn much of who God is, and who we are as well.

Our Mission

One other thing is especially important in the Genesis 1 account. When God determined to create human beings in His own image and likeness He said, "Let them rule . . . over all the earth, and over all the creatures" (Genesis 1:26). Some have twisted this verse to equate *rule* with *exploit*. But the Hebrew word used here, *radah*, found 25 times in the Old Testament, indicates responsibility placed squarely on human beings. We are responsible to uphold all that we, like God, find good in His world.

It is particularly important for us to grasp this if we are to understand the basic nature of spiritual warfare. The Bible pictures Satan as an evil being who is intent on stealing, killing and destroying (see John 10:10). His goal is to corrupt good with evil. But God, in creating human beings in His image and in giving us responsibility for His creation, calls us to overcome Satan's evil—and evil of every kind—with good.

This is a theme we will see again and again as we expose Satan's strategies and learn how to respond to them. As

God's representatives, those who bear the divine image and who, through faith in Jesus, have become God's own sons and daughters, we are called to defeat evil with good. And we are to remember that good can and will overcome evil.

In a sense, we should see the creation of Adam and Eve as God's establishment of a beachhead in Satan's realm. The Bible hints that, even before the first battle, earth was important to Satan. Ezekiel's words, which are addressed to the great fallen angel before the events of Genesis 1, say: "You were in Eden, the garden of God" (Ezekiel 28:13). Today the Bible pictures "the whole world [being] under the control of the evil one" (1 John 5:19). No wonder Jesus did not deny Satan's claim of authority to give power to whomever he chose (see Matthew 4:8–9). Apparently in casting Satan down to earth, God allowed Satan to retain control of our planet.

What crushing irony this must have been for a being whose goal was to supplant God and gain control of the entire universe! How galling it must have been to Satan and his followers—being limited to a tiny planet circling a minor sun in one of some hundred million galaxies!

But even here God would not leave Satan alone. God stripped away the comforting darkness and the chaos of the war-ravaged world and filled it with light and life. And then God created humans in His own image, calling on them to rule, to preserve and establish good throughout the world.

Satan responded quickly to God's challenge.

Satan's Response

Satan's response is described in Genesis 3. He set out to neutralize what might be called God's "secret weapon": human beings. Satan would undermine humankind's original relationship with God, and then use humans to further evil rather than good.

Satan's ploy seemed at first to be successful. Satan sowed confusion about what God had said (see Genesis 3:1), charged bluntly that God's words were lies (see verse 4), and raised doubts about God's motives (see verse 5). Eve, left to rely on the evidence of her senses and on guesses about the outcome of her choices, ate fruit from a tree God had denied them (see verse 6). Then Adam, who unlike Eve fully understood what was involved (see 1 Timothy 2:14), also ate. Adam and Eve had declared their independence from God. They had abandoned relationship with Him, and abandoned their mission.

On the surface it looked as though Satan had won. But when God appeared in the Garden to announce the consequences of the first pair's choice, He said to Satan: "Because you have done this, . . . I will put enmity between you and the woman, between your offspring and hers; he will crush your head, and you will strike his heel" (Genesis 3:14–15). In some yet unexplained way, final victory over Satan and his hordes would be won by a human being, an offspring not of Adam, but of Eve.

From that point on, we human beings have had a choice. Today we can, through faith in Jesus, return to God's fold and become warriors in the invisible war. Or we can continue as lost and wandering individuals, citizens of Satan's kingdom, making choices that support Satan's agenda.

This is, in fact, the most significant decision that everyone has to make. Will I reverse the choice made in Eden? Will I surrender my independence? Will I affirm the truth of God's Word and trust Him fully? And the next decision is, Will I commit to the mission of defeating the powers of darkness?

2

Good vs. Evil

Romans 12:21 provides a pointed summary of the central issue in spiritual warfare. Paul writes: "Do not be overcome by evil, but overcome evil with good."

We are not used to thinking of spiritual warfare in terms of good and evil. We tend to focus on personal conflicts with evil spirits who are intent on oppressing us. Most of the literature on spiritual warfare emphasizes how to defend ourselves against demons and how to cast them out. Yet on a cosmic scale, good and evil are constantly at war in our lives, in our cultures and in our institutions. We are always in danger of good being overcome by evil.

Ever since Satan's defeat in the initial battle, he has had one primary war aim. Satan could not defeat the Creator in open battle, so he marshals evil in an attempt to overwhelm the good that God intended when He created the universe. As spiritual warriors in the conflict between God and the devil, we are called to counter Satan's efforts, and to overcome evil with good.

Scripture's View of Evil

Both the Hebrew of the Old Testament and the Greek of the New have distinctive terms for *evil*. A single family of Hebrew words brings the Old Testament's view of evil into focus. Words in this family are variously translated as "to be evil or bad" or more commonly "to act wickedly" or "to harm." It is important to understand that, in the Old Testament, evil is not an abstract quality. Primarily, evil describes actions, actions that violate God's deep concern for human beings.

One striking aspect of the Old Testament's view of evil is summed up in a wondering remark made by Aaron, Moses' brother: "How prone these people are to do evil!" (Exodus 32:22). Aaron saw clearly the tendency of human beings to act wickedly. But neither he nor Moses ever asked why. For them, evil simply *was*, and was expressed in choices that violate God's essential nature as good, choices that harm others and ourselves.

The harmful effects of evil actions are expressed in the feminine noun in this family of words. Where the feminine noun occurs, it focuses our attention on the pain and misery that result from evil actions. Thus, the feminine noun is translated by words like "harm," "distress," "disaster," "calamity," "trouble," "ruin" and "destruction." It is impossible to understand Scripture's view of evil without sensing the physical and psychological trauma, the personal disasters, that result from evil actions.

The Old Testament is clearly focused on human choice. This is seen in Moses' words to the people of his time: "See, I set before you today life and prosperity [*tob*, "good"], death and destruction [*ra'*, "evil"]" (Deuteronomy 30:15). However limited our ability to choose may be, we are to make choices that will lead us and others to life and prosperity, and protect us and them from death and destruction. This is why we must have a very clear understanding of both good and evil if we are to be effective in spiritual warfare. There is great danger in confusing the two. As Isaiah warns: "Woe to those who call evil good and good evil, who put darkness for light and light for darkness, who put bitter for sweet and sweet for bitter" (Isaiah 5:20). Satan will try every stratagem to confuse us, and so neutralize our contribution to the invisible but very real spiritual warfare going on all around us.

When we turn to the New Testament we find two different word groups used to express the idea of evil. While the two are synonyms, they have different shades of meaning. *Kakos*, with its derivatives, presents evil in a more passive way. Despite being translated by such words and phrases as "wickedness," "malice," "to do harm" and "to do evil," *kakos* is essentially an absence of those qualities that make a person or thing what it should be.

In Romans 7:7–25 Paul explores what it means for a human being to be evil in this sense. Paul recognizes the good that is expressed in God's revelation of His will, and he agrees with God's verdict. But Paul finds himself not doing the good he wants to do, but rather the evil (*kakos*) he does not want to do. There is a flaw that warps every human's nature, causing us to fall short of what we should and even want to be. Satan is well aware of this flaw, and does everything he can to exploit it for evil. But God is also aware of the flaw and, as Paul points out in Romans 8, provides His Holy Spirit to enable us to live truly good and righteous lives.

About half the time, words in the *kakos* family are used to translate words in the Hebrew family. The rest of the time words in another family of Greek words, the *poneros* group, are used to render the Hebrew words. There is a distinct shade of difference between *kakos* and *poneros*. Words in this second group present evil in a stronger, far more active way. The difference is particularly clear when we realize that *poneros* is used to describe the character of Satan, his continuing rebellion against God and his malevolent hatred of humanity.

Words in the *poneros* group are also translated "evil," "bad," "wicked" and "wickedness." While these words are clearly descriptive of Satan and his actions, the New Testament also ascribes *poneros* evil to human beings who are actively hostile to God and goodness. This kind of evil is different from a character defect or lack. This is the kind of evil Jesus described when He taught that "out of the heart come evil thoughts, murder, adultery, sexual immorality, theft, false testimony, slander" (Matthew 15:19).

Satan's broader strategies and his tactics are primarily intended to twist the good gifts God gives to humankind and manipulate us into doing evil, and, thus, to overcome the good God intends. In spiritual warfare we confront every kind of evil, and in overcoming evil with good, we not only bless others but influence them to move toward, rather than away from, God.

Scripture's View of Good

We all have a relatively clear impression of what it means to say something is "good." "That was such a good supper," we say, pushing back from the table, comfortably full. Or "I had such a good time at your party."

While philosophers struggle to define "the good," I suspect most of us are confident that we can recognize good when we see it. We certainly can distinguish the good from trouble or suffering or chronic illness. But Satan is quick to use what often appears to us as good, by twisting or warping it to accomplish evil.

The words translated "good" in the Old Testament are forms of *tob*. These occur at least 620 times in the Hebrew text, and are translated as "good," "better," "well," "beautiful," "pleasing," "goodness," "prosperity," "happiness" and similar terms. It is obvious that *tob* in its broadest sense points to the attractive, the useful and the desirable. It is important, however, to note that *tob*, "good," also indicates that which is morally right.

In my *New International Encyclopedia of Bible Words* (Zondervan, 1985), I describe the one thing all these usages of *tob* have in common:

> The concept that links all these uses of "good" is evaluation. To determine the good, one must compare things, qualities and actions with other things, qualities and actions. One must contrast the beneficial and the right with other things, qualities and actions that are not beneficial and are wrong.

p. 316

For the writers of the Bible, the only one capable of determining what is truly good is God. Corrupted as humans are by sin, our evaluation of what is morally good and right is incomplete or flawed. This is why Proverbs 14:12 warns: "There is a way that seems right to a man, but in the end it leads to death." We need a better way to evaluate what is good than reliance on our reasoning and emotions. Thus, Moses told the Israelites:

"Do what is right and good *in the* LORD's *sight*, so that it may go well with you" (Deuteronomy 6:18, emphasis added).

Generally, we humans tend to agree with God's verdict about what is good and right. We are not at all surprised by Isaiah's directive to "quit your evil ways. Learn to do good, to be fair, and to help the poor, the fatherless, and widows" (Isaiah 1:16–17 TLB). When we hear, "Be just and fair to all" (Isaiah 56:1 TLB), we know what the prophet means. We agree that the actions described truly are "right and good," whether or not we choose do them.

Yet there is more to recognizing the good and right than evaluation. There is an imperative embedded in the very existence of moral good. Acknowledgment of the good serves as a powerful call to choose to *do* what is good. We cannot meet the good and avoid its demand that we make a choice. In a powerful yet simple statement, the prophet Micah reminds God's people of this fact: "He has showed you, O man, what is good. And what does the LORD require of you? To act justly and to love mercy and to walk humbly with your God" (Micah 6:8).

Living Godly Lives

Good in the New Testament is a translation of one of two Greek words, standing alone or in compounds. Their meanings overlap, and both have been used to translate the Hebrew *tob*. Each of the two words occurs 102 times in the New Testament text, but, again, each word has a distinct shade of meaning. *Kalos* stresses the aesthetic. What is good is beautiful, pleasing and pleasant. *Agathos* stresses the useful or beneficial.

In Romans 12 where Paul urges us to offer ourselves to God as living sacrifices that we be enabled to experience God's "good, pleasing and perfect will," he uses *agathos*. When moral choices are in view, God's will is the path to benefits and blessings. Strikingly, when the New Testament encourages believers to do "good deeds," the text tends to use *kalos*. We are to live in ways that others recognize the beauty in our actions as well as their rightness. No wonder Paul reminds Timothy that church leaders must "have a good [*kalos*] reputation with outsiders" (1 Timothy 3:7).

We see one aspect of the attractiveness that we are to maintain in Paul's reminder to Timothy that "the Lord's servant must not quarrel." Here the Greek *quarrel* depicts a sharp, hostile argument. "Instead," the text goes on, "he must be kind to everyone, able to teach, not resentful. Those who oppose him he must gently instruct" (2 Timothy 2:24–25).

The Old Testament emphasizes the fact that God alone is able to judge whether a contemplated action is morally good or evil. The New Testament reminds us that the things God judges as "good" are not only right and beneficial, but also beautiful. We believers are called to live godly lives that benefit others and ourselves, and attract rather than repel outsiders. This is the good with which we are able to overcome evil, a good that is at the same time right, beneficial and beautiful. *To emphasize any of these aspects of the good at the expense of the others opens the door for evil to triumph.*

The apostle Paul draws together Scripture's portrait of good and evil in Galatians 5. There he describes "acts of the sinful nature," a phrase that reflects the Old Testament's emphasis on human evil as practical and behavioral. The "obvious" evil acts in Paul's list include "sexual immorality, impurity and debauchery; idolatry and witchcraft; hatred, discord, jealousy, fits of rage, selfish ambition, dissensions, factions and envy; drunkenness, orgies, and the like" (Galatians 5:19–21).

Then Paul goes on to describe the fruit produced by the Holy Spirit in the life of a believer who is undergoing transformation. Significantly, Paul departs from the description of behaviors. Instead he focuses on the inner character produced by an intimate relationship with God. The fruit of the Spirit is character marked by "love, joy, peace, patience, kindness, goodness, faithfulness, gentleness and self-control" (Galatians 5:22). Thus, Paul reminds us that the good to which we are called in Christ is marked not only by doing what is right and benefits others and ourselves, but also by a beauty that reflects the Spirit's work in our lives.

God blesses humankind with gifts that are designed to maintain all that is good in His creation. Satan, unable to defeat God in direct confrontation, sets out to corrupt the good gifts God has provided. On a cosmic scale, Satan wars against God and humans, determined to twist what God intends for good into evil. In Jesus' analogy, Satan comes as a thief, whose sole intent is "to steal and kill and to destroy" (John 10:10). You and I are called to be warriors on a cosmic scale, warriors who are committed to overcoming evil with good.

The apostle John reminds us that "the reason the Son of God appeared was to destroy the devil's work" (1 John 3:8). The word translated "destroy" here is *lyo*, "to undo." The structures Satan has developed through which he seeks to overcome good with evil are crumbling, and we are called to continue undoing the devil's work by overcoming evil with good.

3

The Eternal
Community of Love

When we read through Genesis 1 and 2 we note time after time that God identified the product of His work as "good." It is perhaps surprising, then, to hear God state in Genesis 2 that "it is not good for the man to be alone" (Genesis 2:18). This was something Adam began to realize as he named animal after animal, with each name identifying something of the uniqueness of the creature. Among none of the animals could Adam find what Scripture calls a "suitable helper" for him.

This phrase, rather than indicate subordination, emphasizes equality. The man Adam and the "suitable helper" God was about to provide were to share the same essential identity as persons created in the image and likeness of God Himself (see Genesis 1:26), and together were charged with the care of God's creation. Clearly Adam realized that, when the

Lord fashioned Eve from one of his ribs and brought her to him: "This is now bone of my bones and flesh of my flesh" (Genesis 2:23).

Genesis 1 shows us that God always intended to fashion humanity with two complementary sexes, for in the preview of the events recorded in that chapter, God is said to have "created man in his own image, in the image of God he created him; male and female he created them" (Genesis 1:27).

Two things are especially important to note. When God first announced His intent to create human beings, He said: "Let us make man in *our* image, in *our* likeness" (Genesis 1:26, emphasis added). Only in view of subsequent revelation can we understand that *our*. The God of the Bible is a Trinity, three Persons sharing the same essence, yet distinct as individuals: Father, Son and Holy Spirit. These three exist in perfect harmony and love. In choosing to create human beings in His image, then, God intended to mold an eternal community of love, where human beings could experience the same endless harmony and joy God knows. No wonder it was "not good" for the man to be alone. Adam—just as you and I—needed someone who shared his identity to love and to be loved by.

And so God fashioned Eve, and brought her to Adam. Adam at once realized she was his partner, his lover, his friend and companion: "Bone of my bones and flesh of my flesh."

The description of God walking with the first pair in the cool of the evening (see Genesis 3:8) reminds us that God created humans "in His own image." God, who is love, reached out to extend His love through the humans who would share His image. This does not, of course, suggest that Adam and Eve were gods. Rather, it affirms that we humans share all that makes God and humans alike. We share with God the capacity to think, to feel, to create, to enjoy, to love and respond to love, to discern and to make moral decisions. In charging humans with the care of the world, God commissioned us to support and uphold all that is truly good. In that process we can experience something of what it means to exist in an eternal community of love.

It is this that brings humanity into direct and deadly conflict with Satan, whose burning desire is to pervert and destroy everything that God intended for good. Yet God provides us with gifts to enable us to taste the community of love that is our destiny to enjoy. These gifts . . . the good gifts . . . are the very things that Satan seeks to overcome with evil. The focus of Satan's most devastating attacks on God and the humans God loves is not demonic attacks on individuals, but rather attacks on the gifts through which God enables us to experience today something of the eternal community of love that awaits us when Jesus returns.

In this book we will look at gifts that God has given to help us experience something of the coming eternal community of love. We will look at ways Satan seeks to overcome the good in the gifts by distorting them with evil. And we will explore what each of us, as God's warrior in the cosmic struggle, can do to overcome that evil with good.

What gifts has God provided to enable us to experience something of the eternal community of love in our here and now?

The Gift of Core Community
The Gift of Choice
The Gift of Family
The Gift of the Law
The Gift of a Community of Faith

The Gift of Restoration
The Gift of God's Discipline
The Gift of Uniqueness
The Gift of Provision
The Gift of Truth
The Gift of Peace
The Gift of Eternal Life, Now!
The Gift of Unconditional Acceptance

PART 2

WARFARE IN THE HERE AND NOW

4

The Gift of Core Community

Adam was alone. He possessed all the gifts that being a "person" implies. As persons, we think. We also feel. We create. We appreciate beauty. We enjoy good food. We gain a sense of accomplishment from work well done. For Adam the one empty space in his life was his growing awareness that something was missing. Adam had no one like himself to love and to be loved by. Oh, Adam sensed God's love for him, and responded to that love. But somehow he yearned for something more, something different.

I suspect Adam did not even know what he yearned for until the day God brought Eve to him. Then Adam knew. Then he cried out in joy, "This is now bone of my bones, and flesh of my flesh!" There in the Garden, Adam was united with his wife. And although naked, they felt no shame.

In that first core community of husband and wife, all that counted was that Adam knew and loved Eve and Eve knew and loved Adam. Neither of the two was "alone." In the community they formed, each was fully accepted, loved unconditionally and secure. In their minds there was no sense of "me," but only "us."

Satan's Strategy Exposed

Satan responded immediately. The true goodness experienced in this core community of love somehow had to be overcome by evil. We all know the tactics of deception he used. Satan focused his attention on Eve, while a silent Adam observed. Gradually, Satan led Eve to uncertainty about what God had said. Then Satan denied the truth of God's words, and went on to plant doubts about God's motives into Eve's heart.

No longer trusting God, Eve was left to herself to decide what to do. The fruit looked ripe. It smelled fragrant and was probably tasty. And eating it might, as Satan suggested, make her wise. So Eve went with her instincts, took a bite of the fruit and then offered it to Adam.

Commenting millenniums later, the apostle Paul notes that Eve was deceived. But Adam knew exactly what he was doing (see 1 Timothy 2:14). Throughout the Scriptures it is Adam's sin that is identified as bringing about the fall of our race, not Eve's.

What was the difference between Adam's sin and Eve's? Eve was deceived. She did not understand the core issue involved in disobeying God. Adam was not deceived. He knew what was implied in disobeying God. In eating the forbidden fruit, Adam chose independence from the Lord; to do what he wanted to do when he chose to do it, to determine for himself what might help him and what might harm him. Adam rejected God's warnings, and turned to a life that would truly be lived alone. From then on he would have a life lived by and for "me."

But while Adam knew the choice he was making, he had no idea of the consequences.

The Immediate Consequences

Genesis 3:8–13 describes the immediate consequences of Adam and Eve's disobedience. When God visited them in the evening they did not meet Him as "us." Adam felt shame and fear and tried to hide from God. When confronted with his sin, Adam pointed to Eve and said, "The woman you put here with me—she gave me some fruit from the tree" (3:12). When God turned to Eve, she had her own excuse: "The serpent deceived me" (3:13).

There is no "us" here. No budding core community of love. There are only two isolated "me's"—an Adam, and an Eve—each thinking only of himself or herself, each trying desperately to shift responsibility to the other.

The core community that God gave humans in which to experience something of the eternal community of love was shattered. God's good had been overcome by evil.

The Lasting Consequences

After pronouncing a curse on Satan (see Genesis 3:14–15), God then explained the lasting consequences of the choice of independence for women (see verse 16) and for men (see verses 17–19). Women, left to face life as "me," sensing the loss of "us," will seek desperately to please men. But they will discover that the men they look to for security will exploit and rule over them. Women will bear children, but both the process of giving birth and the experience of seeing their children grow up as "me's," as selfish and independent as their parents, will sear a woman's heart with pain. And rather than look to God for relief, women will instead look to the very sex that causes them their deepest anguish.

As for men, their "me" focus will be on work and on personal achievement. For those who are married, the joy of living life in that "us" relationship with their wives will be ignored, even as the necessity for a personal relationship with God will seem less and less relevant in view of the challenges of making a living here on this earth.

And godly singles will find it more and more difficult to connect with life partners who also seek this core commitment of "us."

Reading early Genesis and the account of the Fall, it would seem, as we have noted, that Satan triumphed. The good that God intended in establishing marriage as the core community, an intimate community in which partners are given a taste of the eternal community of love, has been twisted and corrupted by evil into a relationship often causing overwhelming pain rather than providing a foretaste of joy.

Overcoming Evil with Good

The picture drawn in Genesis 3 of the relationship between husbands and wives, the core community, is a dark one. Everywhere we look there is more and more evidence of Satan's distortion of male-female relationships. Young girls beg for push-up bras, and dress sexually to attract the attention of hormone-driven teenage boys. Print and media ads draw attention by featuring semi-naked women. All too common sexual abuse, abductions and rapes underscore how women have been refashioned in the eyes of men into mere sex objects; they are "its" for the masculine world's "me's" to use and discard. In America physical violence in male-female relationships is near an all-time high. One recent research project showed that more than 30 percent of men have struck the women with whom they are in a relationship—and that some 27 percent of women have struck their male companions.

It is against this grim portrait of our society that we view the words of Scripture: "Do not be overcome by evil, but overcome evil with good" (Romans 12:21).

God is not saying, "Go out and change the world." Nor is He telling us to tear away the shroud of evil that Satan has cast over our world (see 1 John 5:19). We know that in Christ's cross the decisive blow against evil has already been struck. It is the fact that Christ came to destroy (tear down) the devil's work that shows us how we are to conduct spiritual warfare on this level. Married couples are to overcome the evil Satan has done *to their own core communities* with good. Husbands and wives are to work together to tear down the work Satan has done and repair their own core communities of love.

Too Many Solutions?

Today there are almost too many books on Christian marriage. On the Internet you can find ads for "*The* [italics mine] 7 Secrets to Fixing Your Marriage," and other books about how "headship" in marriage is supposed to work, including exhortations that "unselfish" headship be exercised by the husband. Still others suggest that while husband and wife are "partners," it is necessary to remember that Eve was created as a "helper" (that is, subordinate to Adam). This is an interpretation of the phrase *suitable helper* that significantly distorts the meaning and use of the Hebrew *'etzer* (see Psalm 118:7). In yet another approach, one author suggests that Adam's headship indicates not that Adam was called to rule over Eve, "but to lead her in submitting to God's rule."

To this we can add various approaches affirming "equality" in marriage that can be maintained by assigning different roles to husbands and to wives. To some this means he earns the money and handles the checkbook. To others it means the husband and wife exchange leadership in areas of their differing gifts and abilities. He struggles with math, so she handles the checkbook. Each of these various approaches is then used not only to generate a definition of what a healthy Christian marriage is, but also to define what each partner in a marriage is supposed to (or is allowed to) do.

Jesus' Words about Marriage

I grow concerned when I read the typical book about Christian marriage because of an incident reported in the gospels. Jesus was challenged by a group of Pharisees who asked Him about divorce. "Is it lawful for a man to divorce his wife for any and every reason?" they asked (Matthew 19:3). Jesus did not allow Himself to be drawn into the contemporary argument concerning valid grounds for divorce. Instead Jesus responded,

"Haven't you read," he replied, "that at the beginning the Creator 'made them male and female,' and said, 'For this reason a man will leave his father and mother and be united to his wife, and the two will become one flesh'? So they are no longer two, but one."

Matthew 19:4–6

What is significant is that Christ *looked back, past the Fall, and spoke of marriage as it was "at the beginning."* Then the two were one—an "us" rather than two "me's" coming together in the hope that the needs of each individual would be met by the other. In the beginning there were no consequences like those initiated by the Fall, no man claiming the right to rule over the woman. Yes, after the Fall many husbands and wives have loved each other dearly, and done the best they could. But Jesus calls us in Matthew 19 to go back to the beginning; back to the time when the two became one flesh. If we are to recover the core community, in which husband and wife experience life as one, we must go back with Jesus to the beginning.

My Imperfect Marriage

When I married Sue some 31 years ago, I expected a perfect marriage. We loved each other. We had talked through issues that trouble most marriages, and felt we were in total agreement. But the one thing I had not done was go back before the Fall. Despite never intending to "rule over" my wife, I came to assume that I had a clearer perspective on things than she did. This did not lead to conflict. I continued to be a "nice guy." She kept on being loving, despite her deep disappointment. I was not controlling about our home; she had freedom to furnish and arrange the house as she desired. And I was proud of her gift as a Bible teacher and educator.

But if there was something she suggested we do, something that for some reason I did not want to do, we usually ended up doing it my way. Like the time the outside of our new house was being painted. Sue had specified the color peach, and when she saw the paint was actually pastel pink, she was upset. The contract said peach, and she wanted peach. The paint looked peachy enough for me, though, and I failed to back her up when she wanted to insist on the peach originally specified. For years driving up to our home was a reminder of how casually I had dismissed her wishes.

And I failed to support her desire after she retired from teaching to go for an advanced degree. After many years I realized that not only had I taken on the role of benevolent dictator in our home, but also in dozens of ways I had been dismissive of her wants and needs. It was a terrible thing to discover about myself. But the real damage had been done to Sue. I had made her feel so dismissed and unimportant over the years that she had lost not only the joy of life but also a sense of who she was as a unique person.

Unwittingly, I had carried our marriage beyond the Fall, to live with her as a separate "me," rather than nurturing the "us" relationship that is essential to experiencing marriage as a reflection of the core community of love.

As I have studied the Genesis "before" and "after" descriptions of the marriage relationship, I have come to believe that the most significant passages on marriage in the epistles do just what Jesus did when challenged by the Pharisees. Christ went back before the Fall and spoke of what it was like "at the beginning."

The Question of Submission

Few passages in Scripture on the subject of marriage are mis-interpreted more than Paul's comments on submission, which are often used to suppress women. His teaching begins in Ephesians 5:21, where he writes: "Submit to one another out of reverence for Christ." Within the next few verses specific relationships are singled out: wives submit to husbands, the Church submits to Christ (see Ephesians 5:22–24). A similar emphasis is placed on love in Ephesians 5:25–30. Husbands are to love their wives as Christ loves the Church. And then Paul sets his discussion in the context of marriage as it existed before the Fall, by quoting Genesis 2:24.

Too often the mention of headship (see Ephesians 5:23) is assumed to refer to marriage *after* the Fall. But here, as in other passages, *head* can mean "source," as in the phrase "head [source] of the river." When we place Paul's discussion of marriage in the context he himself references—by quoting from Genesis 2:24 to sum up his argument—we see that the sense in which *head* is used here is not hierarchical, as if the man were "over" the woman. It affirms the simple historical fact that Adam *was* the source of Eve, and that Christ through His sacrifice on the cross became the source of the Church, which is His Body (Ephesians 5:23).

If *head* is used in the sense of "source" here, what is the sense of *submit*—especially when Paul begins with the command, "Submit to one another"?

Submit as used in the Bible is a complex term, with many shades of emphasis. Submission can be coerced, and submission can be voluntary. Voluntary submission can be motivated simply by one's culture's view of the right thing to do. Or voluntary submission might be motivated by one's convictions concerning right and wrong. It is clear in this passage that Paul is speaking of voluntary submission. But it is equally clear that this voluntary submission is interpersonal, a response to another person. In fact, in this context we might go so far as to translate *submit* as "respond." Wives are to respond to their husbands as the Church is to respond to Christ. And again, as Paul emphasizes at the beginning of this passage, we are to "submit [that is, be responsive] to each other out of reverence for Christ."

With this understanding we can go back to Genesis 2 and describe what it is like for a man and a woman to fashion . . . and experience . . . that core community of love that Satan has been so eager to overcome with evil.

Life Together Before the Fall

From Genesis and Ephesians we can identify several characteristics of what life in the core community, marriage, is to be like.

First, Adam and Eve were equals, each sharing fully in the image and likeness of God. Neither was superior; neither "ruled over" the other.

Second, the two were equally responsible to care for God's creation and to maintain what was good.

Third, Adam expressed his love for Eve by actively encouraging the development of her gifts and talents. We see this reflected in Christ's desire that His Church be "radiant . . . , without stain or wrinkle or any other blemish, but holy and blameless" (Ephesians 5:27). Christ does everything He can to make sure that the Church becomes everything she can be. In the same way, husbands are to do everything they can to see that their wives become everything they can be.

Fourth, Adam and Eve were totally accepted by each other, safe and secure in each other's love.

Fifth, Adam and Eve were naked but not ashamed. Each fully exposed himself or herself to the other, aware of any flaws, but confident of the other's love and unconditional acceptance. Each was eager to know the other's thoughts and feelings.

I am sure there is much more that we do not know about the relationship of Adam and Eve before the Fall. But what we can tell from Scripture is enough to enable us to overcome much evil in personal core relationships. That is the challenge set before husbands and wives.

If you are married, or plan to marry, be aware that Satan will attempt to overcome the good in your relationship with evil. And be committed to overcome the evil he seeks to do with good.

Nurturing the Core Community

1. Remain completely committed to each other.
2. Accept and appreciate each other fully.
3. Express your thoughts and feelings freely.
4. Welcome your spouse's expression of thoughts and feelings.
5. Listen attentively to what the other is saying.
6. Pray together about important issues and for one another.
7. Tell your partner when you feel dismissed or uncared for.
8. Tell your partner when you feel loved and valued.
9. Talk about what would help you feel more fulfilled as a person.
10. Confess sins and negative thoughts freely.

11. Forgive one another wholeheartedly.

12. Identify and affirm your spouse's strengths and gifts.

13. Tell your partner often what you appreciate about him or her.

14. Dream together about your future.

15. Set aside time to share in activities you both enjoy.

16. Encourage each other to work toward achieving personal goals.

17. Commit to making love with your spouse frequently.

18. Touch and hold your spouse daily.

5

The Gift of Choice

At first glance "choice" does not look much like a gift. We might even mistake it for a curse. As the story in Genesis opens we see a blissfully happy couple living in a beautiful garden where everything is provided for them. There is no struggle to survive; fruits, grains, vegetables and melons abound. There is no danger from wild animals; Adam has named and is familiar with them all. Best of all, God visits in the cool of the evening, to walk and talk with them. There is no reason why this situation might not continue endlessly, not only for Adam and Eve, but also for their children and their children's children. After all, God's intent in creating humans in His own image and likeness was to love and be loved by them. And the final chapters in the last book of the Bible, Revelation, portray a redeemed humanity living with the Creator in just this kind of eternal community of love.

But for one thing. In creating Adam and Eve God provided them the capacity to choose. In Ephesians 2:1–3 the apostle Paul describes graphically the condition brought about by Adam and Eve's choice.

> You were dead in your transgressions and sins, in which you used to live when you followed the ways of this world and of the ruler of the kingdom of the air, the spirit who is now at work in those who are disobedient. All of us also lived among them at one time, gratifying the cravings of our sinful nature and following its desires and thoughts.

Their choice brought spiritual death, made us vulnerable to the schemes of Satan, and awoke sinful desires and thoughts that have been passed on to "all of us." No wonder some question whether God's gift of the ability to choose was a good gift, or a curse.

A Necessary Gift

Yet it is clear that the ability to choose was a necessary gift. This is spelled out for us in the Bible's first mention of human beings, in Genesis 1:26.

> Then God said, "Let us make man in our image, in our likeness, and let them rule over the fish of the sea and the birds of the air, over the livestock, over all the earth, and over all the creatures that move along the ground."

God's intent was to "make man" (human beings) in His own image and likeness. Since God is a person, to be stamped with His image and likeness required that humans be persons, too. And to be persons rather than puppets, we had to be given the ability to choose. If we were truly to bear the image and likeness of God, it was impossible *not* to create us with the gift of choice.

There is another hint in Genesis 1:26 why the gift of choice was necessary. God stated His intention of letting humans "rule over" what we today would call the biosphere—all areas on the earth that support life. The Hebrew word for *rule* here is *radah*. It occurs 25 times in the Old Testament, and is used to indicate the rule of human beings rather than the rule of God.

Even before God created human beings, His intent was to entrust the welfare of earth and its living creatures to humankind. To carry out this mission, human beings must be able to distinguish between options, and be able to choose the best. Choice is a gift God simply had to give to humankind. Without the ability to choose we would not be persons as God is a person. Without the ability to choose we would never be able to care for God's creation.

The Light Fades

I have suggested that Satan, who lost the decisive initial battle in his war with the Creator, then set about to overcome with evil the good that God intended. Nowhere in Scripture is this clearer than in the experience of Adam and Eve in Eden. Satan went to them, undermined Eve's trust in God and His motives, and then held out the possibility of something that *seemed* good, moving Eve to disobey God. Adam, with more insight into the significance of disobeying God, also used his ability to choose to disobey God in favor of an illusory independence.

With that choice, the light that shone so brightly in Eden faded, and Adam and Eve began to realize what they had done. Then the Lord God stepped into the Garden, and explained the lasting consequences of this first choice. Satan had won this battle, but he could claim only temporary victory. Adam and Eve, and all their offspring, *retained the ability to choose!* As the Bible's story unfolds we see how vital that ability to choose remains.

A Clear Choice

The next event recorded in Genesis helps us clarify the basic issue we all face in using God's gift of choice.

Adam and Eve's two sons sought to approach God. Abel, who tended sheep, brought a prime animal to sacrifice. Cain, who farmed, brought the best of his produce. God accepted Abel's sacrifice, but rejected Cain's. Cain's reaction was anger, and the text says that "his face was downcast."

God then spoke to Cain and said, "If you do what is right, will you not be accepted?" (Genesis 4:7). Cain knew what was right. After Adam and Eve had sinned, God had killed two animals and made "garments of skin for Adam and his wife and clothed them" (3:21). This first blood sacrifice, made to cover those who had sinned, foreshadowed the animal sacrifices that became an essential element in Israel's worship, and pointed to Jesus' sacrifice of Himself on Calvary. The phrase *If you do what is right* makes it perfectly clear that Cain knew he should bring a blood sacrifice. But Cain wanted God to accept the best that Cain could do on his own.

After God promised to accept Cain if he did "what was right," Cain lured his brother into the field and murdered him.

It is a terrible story, but not an unfamiliar one. We live in a world where anger and hostility drive individuals and whole cultures into murderous rages. All too often the innocent suffer because of choices made by others. In a world where such horrors exist, it is hard for us not to assume that Satan has won, and has turned the gift of choice to his own evil ends. But, again, we are not called to change the world. Jesus will do that when He returns. Our part in the invisible war is to overcome Satan's evil with good today, wherever we can. And God's words to Cain clarify how.

> Then the LORD said to Cain, "Why are you angry? Why is your face downcast? If you do what is right, will you not be accepted? But if you do not do what is right, sin is crouching at your door; it desires to have you, but you must master it."
>
> Genesis 4:6–7

Sin is always crouching at the door, eager to take us in its grip. We "master" sin by using the gift of choice that God has given us. We overcome evil by choosing to "do what is right."

What Is "Right"?

At this point, some are sure to argue that we do not always know the right thing to do. If we are speaking of personal choices that have no moral element, that is true. Should I apply to college or join the navy? is a personal question. And the answer to such questions will be different for each individual.

God's encouragement of Cain to do "what is right," however, is very different. God had established a standard that

Cain needed to meet. Where there are standards established by God, we *do* know "what is right."

It is a striking truth that a person does not have to be a believer to know what is right. In Romans 3:2 Paul celebrates the fact that the Jewish people have in Scripture "the very words of God." He also reminds us that Gentiles, meaning here those who do not have the Law, still have moral standards. Paul is saying that even unbelievers "do by nature things required by the law" (Romans 2:14). Paul is pointing out that God created humans as moral beings. Whatever culture we explore, whatever era we visit, we find that people see the same kinds of things as moral issues. The way we treat others, sexual practices and property rights are everywhere viewed as moral issues. One's conscience not only identifies the right thing for a person to do, but also accuses if he or she does not do what is right.

This does not mean that the standards in every society mirror biblical standards. Specific rules differ from culture to culture. But awareness that certain issues are moral in nature has been implanted in us by the Creator. Every one of us recognizes "right" and "not right."

Satan's Strategy Exposed

Satan's strategies to nudge us toward choosing what is not right are hardly new or innovative. But they are effective.

He uses two major tactics in Western culture. *The first tactic* is to encourage relativism. This is the assumption that there is no such thing as absolute truth or absolute morality. A thing can be true for one person and not true for another. Or an action might be morally right for one person and morally wrong for another. Each individual determines for himself or herself what is right and what is not right. But without an external standard that defines what is right, "right" and "wrong" are nothing more than personal opinions. Without an external standard, there is no reliable moral compass to guide our use of God's gift of choice. Where relativism dominates, evil is sure to overcome good.

Even Christians who are confident that God has spoken to us in His Word can become confused in a relativistic culture. Satan's question to Eve in the Garden is especially relevant for us: "Did God really say . . . ?" (Genesis 3:1). Where so many competing ideas of what is right and what is not right abound, it is vital that we check out carefully what God really *did* say.

The second tactic is reflected in something called situation ethics. Jesus taught that we must love our neighbors as ourselves. Christian proponents of situation ethics have argued from Jesus' teaching that in any situation we simply determine "the loving thing to do," and choose that. If doing the loving thing means we have to break one of God's Ten Commandments, then that is what we must do.

The major problem with situation ethics is that what is right and what is not right are not simply a matter of motives. Our intentions might be good, but we cannot predict the results of our choices. In fact, situation ethics leads us back to Eden. Eve chose to eat the forbidden fruit not only because "it was pleasing to the eye," but also, primarily, because it was "desirable for gaining wisdom." Eve chose to do what was not right because she thought it would lead to something "good."

Eve could not have been more wrong. Whatever her motive, the choice she made led to disaster. We recall the words from Proverbs: "There is a way that seems right to a man, but in the end it leads to death" (Proverbs 14:12).

The more we explore the gift of choice, the more we see its downside. The choices Adam and Eve made in the Garden brought disaster on our entire human population. Today, too, Satan schemes to overcome the good we intend with evil. He has shaped a culture of relativism, and by suggesting that the outcome we intend defines what is right and what is not right, Satan leaves us to wander in a world filled with unintended consequences. In time, even our nagging consciences are silenced.

Overcoming Evil with Good

As we read through the Bible, we realize that God has given us another gift to accompany the gift of choice. He has revealed *what is right*, and encourages us to do *what is right in His eyes*. Deuteronomy 6:24 reminds us that "the LORD commanded us to obey all these decrees and to fear the LORD our God, so that we might always prosper." God is eager to bless us, and the path to blessing is to do what is right in His sight, not in our own sight or in the sight of our culture.

In a sense God's standards are both a blessing and a curse. God makes it very clear that hewing to what He says is right makes a difference. There is blessing "if you obey the commands of the LORD" and a "curse if you disobey the commands of the LORD" (Deuteronomy 11:27–28). Today we might say something like: Doing what is right in His eyes helps, while doing what is not right in His eyes harms.

If God had not shown us the path to what helps us rather than harms us, choice would not be a good gift at all. But

God has revealed what is right and what is not right, and He supervises the outcomes of our choices.

A "Prosperity Gospel"?

We noted earlier Moses' prophetic words in Deuteronomy 30:15: "See, I set before you today life and prosperity, death and destruction." God was teaching the nation of Israel that those who walk in His ways and keep His commandments will "live and increase, and the LORD your God will bless you" (verse 16). Words of promise such as these are sometimes distorted to promote a "prosperity gospel": Do what is right in God's sight, and He will bless you with wealth, health, a happy marriage and obedient children.

It is true that we are far better off when we choose to do what is right rather than choose to do what is not right. But there is no guarantee that doing what is right will bring wealth or happiness. The apostle Peter points out that normally a person committed to doing good will "see good days." But in the unusual case where we do what is right and suffer for it, God has a special purpose in it. After all, Jesus did no wrong and was crucified. But His death resulted in bringing us to God (see 1 Peter 3:8–22).

The point here is that we are called to do what is right. Period. It is up to God to supervise the results of our choices. Again, we are to focus on what is right, and not make decisions based on what we hope—or fear—will result from the choices we make.

This is the lesson that is so clear in God's words to Cain. There was only one decision to be made. Cain needed to choose to do what was right rather than choose to do what was not right. Only the choice of what was right would enable Cain to master the sin that was crouching at the door, eager to have him. Cain surrendered to sin, and murdered his brother. He made the wrong choice, and tragedy ensued. What we learn from the story of Cain is that whatever choices we face, we need to concentrate on doing what is right in God's eyes.

Benefits of the Right Choice

Our lives are made up of a series of seemingly insignificant choices. But each little choice moves us a little further down one of two paths. We can do what is right, and take a step toward becoming the persons God wants us to be. Or we can do what is not right, and drift further away from God and from our own best selves. It is the choices we make that shape our character, and determine who we will become.

By choosing to do what is right, you and I are doing our part in overcoming evil with good, and we participate in tearing down the kingdom Satan is fighting desperately to preserve.

Living with the Ability to Choose

1. Make a conscious commitment to serve God.
2. Follow up that commitment by evaluating carefully the large and small choices you make daily.
3. Keep your focus on the question, What is the right thing to do?, not on the supposed good you think will result from your choice.
4. Read Scripture, asking God to enable you better to understand and appreciate Him. After all, God's

standards are an expression of His character. The better you know the Lord, the clearer the right thing to do will become.

5. The writer of Hebrews encourages believers to go on to maturity, explaining that the mature are those "who by constant use have trained themselves to distinguish good from evil" (Hebrews 5:14). Train yourself to evaluate the moral basis for your actions.

6. Make sure to use your gift of choice to overcome evil with good.

6

The Gift of Family

The core community, the relationship of husband and wife, was a gift intended to enable a man and a woman to experience together something of the eternal community of love that awaits us at history's end. In God's good plan, as that relationship matures and grows, it becomes the context for another of God's gifts: family. God designed the family so that children born into this world could grow up surrounded and supported by love. As children are born, the family is meant to be a place where children and adults together shape a safe place where they can experience aspects of that perfect community of love that awaits us.

In one of his psalms, Solomon waxes enthusiastic about God's gift of family. Apparently, his motto regarding children was, "The more the merrier": "Sons are a heritage from the LORD, children a reward from him. Like arrows in the hands of a warrior are sons born in one's youth. Blessed is the man whose quiver is full of them" (Psalm 127:3–5).

As we survey the Proverbs, family seems a mixed blessing. On the one hand, "a wise son heeds his father's instruction" (Proverbs 13:1). On the other, "a fool spurns his father's discipline" (Proverbs 15:5). This is especially telling, as the word for *fool* here is *'iwwelet*, which views foolishness as a moral deficiency. The fact is, the family can reflect something of the coming eternal community of love, but foolishness "is bound up in the heart of a child" (Proverbs 22:15). All children, no less than Cain, have been corrupted by the Fall. Each child born into this world still bears the image of the Creator, but that image is deeply flawed.

The image of God stamped on the human personality makes it possible for each of us to overcome evil with good. But the distortion of that image makes it equally possible that we will succumb to Satan's schemes and take a stand with evil against good. The dissolution of the family unit in today's world leaves little doubt as to the success Satan has had in waging war against this gift. But even in homes where the traditional model is securely in place, children can grow into adults who choose to abandon good moral conduct.

Samson, although a leader in Israel, squandered his gift of unusual strength on personal vendettas against the Philistines. Yet it is clear from references to his family in the book of Judges that he had godly parents whose guidance he simply refused to follow.

Hezekiah was one of the godliest of Judah's kings, yet his son Manasseh was perhaps the most evil. Manasseh's actions during his 55-year reign set a moral tone that doomed the nation to deportation by the Babylonians.

Both of these stories told in Scripture underline the fact that individuals are free to choose. While it is clear that parents and legal guardians are responsible to provide the "corrections of discipline" that are "the way to life" (Proverbs 6:23), even that godly influence does not determine the course children will take.

Biblical proverbs are not promises. They state what is most likely to occur. So when we read that "folly is bound up in the heart of a child, but the rod of discipline will drive it far from him" (Proverbs 22:15), we see that parents are encouraged to discipline their children. But this proverb does not guarantee that disciplining children wisely will cause them to become godly men and women.

Pointing the Way

Sayings in the book of Proverbs about training children are reinforced by references in the New Testament (see Ephesians 6:1–4; Colossians 3:20; Hebrews 12:5–6). Both Testaments make it clear that children are to honor mother and father, and to be responsive to—to obey—parental instructions. But for this to happen, perhaps most important of all, children need a safe and secure environment where they experience love and acceptance. To be most effective, this nurture and training of children should take place in a relational context like that described in Deuteronomy 6:5–9:

> Love the LORD your God with all your heart and with all your soul and with all your strength. These commandments that I give you today are to be upon your hearts. Impress them on your children. Talk about them when you sit at home and when you walk along the road, when you lie down and when you get up. Tie them as symbols on your hands and bind them on your foreheads. Write them on the doorframes of your houses and on your gates.

This instruction is repeated almost word for word in Deuteronomy 11:18–20:

> Fix these words of mine in your hearts and minds; tie them as symbols on your hands and bind them on your foreheads. Teach them to your children, talking about them when you sit at home and when you walk along the road, when you lie down and when you get up. Write them on the doorframes of your houses and on your gates.

The repetition, as with all repetition in Scripture, serves to emphasize the importance of the instruction. Training and discipline are to be done *informally, in the context of experiences shared with the rest of the family*.

Essential Elements

These two passages from Deuteronomy bring into focus three essential elements that enable the members of a family to experience something of that eternal Kingdom of love as they live together.

The first essential element is to love the Lord "with all your heart and with all your soul and with all your strength." Parents who are committed to the Lord and are growing in their relationship with Him set a Kingdom tone for the other family members.

When I was teaching at Wheaton College, I assigned one of my graduate classes a research project at the Wheaton Christian Grammar School with eighth graders. Our goal was to see if we could determine whether or not God was real to the students, and if so, what factor or factors promoted a sense of the reality of God. The students were asked to use crayons to draw pictures of what they felt God was like. We then asked them to describe their pictures, and wrote down the words they used. When we analyzed the pictures and descriptions, it was clear that some of the boys and girls felt very positive about God and close to Him. It was also clear that some experienced God as distant, and somewhat threatening.

Then we administered a questionnaire. We asked about family devotions, discipline, Bible reading and other practices encouraged in many Christian homes. What we found was surprising. The single factor that influenced whether or not one of our eighth graders felt close to God was his or her perception of how real God was to Mom and Dad. In every case where the child reported that God was real to his or her parents, that child had a sense of his or her own connection with the Lord. And in every case where the child reported that he did not think God was real to his parents, that child sensed God as distant, and often threatening.

If children are to be nurtured in a context where they experience something of God's love, those who care for them must experience God's love for themselves.

The second essential element for a family to experience the eternal Kingdom of love is expressed by these verses: "These commandments that I give you today are to be upon your hearts" (Deuteronomy 6:6), and "Fix these words of mine in your hearts and minds" (Deuteronomy 11:18). Parents should know God's Word and take it to heart. They are to grasp His priorities and values and make them their own. They are to live the truth they understand, and to be on a quest constantly to learn more.

The third essential element is to teach God's Word in a *nonformal* setting. In our culture, teaching or instruction is considered to be what happens in school. The problem is that what is learned in formal settings is seldom integrated into one's life. And it almost never has an impact on one's values, personal commitments or lifestyle. It is in nonformal settings, in the process of sharing life, that hearts and minds are shaped.

Satan's Strategy Exposed

Some statistics regarding American households show how successful Satan has been at preempting the optimal family unit that God designed. "Family" is viewed less and less as two parents providing a safe haven within which children can be nurtured, gain a sense of who God is and find a personal relationship with Him. More children, for instance, are born to unmarried mothers than at any time in our history. According to the Pew Research Center, in 1960 just 5 percent of all births were to unmarried women. In 2011, that number had risen to 41 percent. When broken down by races, we see that 72 percent of births among black women were to unmarried mothers; 53 percent among Hispanic women; and 29 percent among white women. Checking another statistic, we see that in 1960, 37 percent of all American households included a married couple raising their own children. Today this pattern includes just 16 percent of households.

Tragically, there is very little the individual Christian can do to stem the fast-flowing tide of cultural trends away from the original concept of the family unit. How is Satan able to overcome the good in God's gift of family? If we use the United States as a test case, I see three major strategies Satan uses to have a negative impact on the family unit.

The first tactic is to isolate age groups. Age grading has permeated our society. It is natural, of course, for children to play with age mates, and they should be encouraged to take part in activities appropriate to their ages. But as they enter the school years, children usually become grouped to the point that their only significant contacts are with children of the same age. Classrooms are geared to specific age levels. Then after school, whether it is Sunday school or soccer camp, almost everything a child does in contact with others tends to be organized by age.

While this way of grouping children might seem logically to be the most efficient, its pervasiveness limits any significant contact children have with adults or older children who might serve as role models. This is a particular loss in the area of Christian role models—those who express love for the Lord in their daily lives. It is in the day-to-day settings that faith is both taught and caught through the lives of those who love God and pattern their lives by His Word.

The second tactic Satan uses is to fill the lives of parents so that they have little quality time to spare for their boys and girls. It is understandable in an economy where most parents must both work to meet family expenses, take care of household chores, and still find time for each other and for rest, that there is little energy to invest in relationships with children. One study reveals, however, that in the United States fathers spend only about ten minutes a day with their children! While other studies offer more encouraging results, few measure the kinds of interactions moms and dads might optimally have with their young boys and girls or adolescents. It is ironic that other studies show that adults in our society spend at least *four hours a day* sitting in front of the television.

A *third tactic* of Satan is to encourage the use of media as a substitute for personal relationships. Computers, cell phones, texting, Facebook and Twitter have been adopted by even young children. While most in the younger generations eagerly collect "friends," they interact with few face-to-face. This is particularly deadly for building relationships, because much of significance is communicated through body language—tone of voice, facial expression, etc. Texting, the preferred method of communication for teens and twenties, limits the data that can be communicated and tends to keep relationships on a superficial level. No wonder Sherry Turkle in *Alone Together* (Basic Books, 2012) points out that as we expect more from technology, we expect less from each other.

I am not suggesting here that there are no advantages in age grading, no benefits in meeting the economic needs of the family and no value in competence in the use of media. What I am suggesting is that Satan has been quick to grasp the potential for each of these cultural shifts in order to distort the good God intended when He placed us in families.

We are unlikely to change the directions in which our culture is moving. But we can recognize the dangers and take steps in our own areas of influence to overcome evil with good.

Overcoming Evil with Good

Deuteronomy 6 and 11 picture closely knit families. Parents love the Lord and live by His Word. They share much of life with their children. And they surround the family with symbols reminding them all of God's presence. Ideally, parents explain the choices they make by referring the whole family to God's Word. It might seem challenging to reproduce this kind of family life in our busy, fragmented 21st century. And it is. Yet as I reread these passages and think of Satan's strategies I cannot help remembering events in the experience of my own family that countered his schemes.

During the time our two boys were in the formative years I traveled about a third of the time. But when I was not on the road, I made sure to spend time with them. We played half-court basketball in the backyard nearly every day, often with neighborhood young people. When my oldest was about eight, I noticed that he hesitated to go into a dark room. I suggested we write a book together about fear. Paul decided to title it *Paul's Not Being Afraid Book*. I read various verses about fear and trust from a concordance, and he selected the verses he liked. I typed them and pasted them into a book form, which Paul then illustrated. One featured Daniel being thrown into a den of fierce lions, and the verse was, "What time I am afraid I will trust in You." I never did mention Paul's fear of the dark. I did not have to. As Paul explored fear and trust in his book, the Holy Spirit removed the fear and replaced it with trust.

About this same time, Paul became fascinated with Paul White's *Jungle Doctor* books, about a missionary's adventures in Africa. So every night I sat by his bed and read *Jungle Doctor* stories.

My younger son, Tim, had different interests. I remember he cried when we finished the Narnia series, till I reassured him we could go back and read them again at any time. Later we read *Man in Black*, the biography of Johnny Cash, and, to my surprise, Tim asked we read John Walvoord's commentary *Revelation*.

Some of my happiest memories are of camping and fishing trips with the boys and their friends. Especially significant were the two weeks each year—one in the spring and one in the fall—that I took them out of school so we could go on fishing expeditions. Being out of school made those fishing trips special!

But probably the most important event we shared was when I discovered that a contractor I had hired to work on our backyard had been cheating us. I was upset and angry. Then I remembered Jesus' command to bless those who despitefully use you. I got the family together, told them what had happened and explained that I was still going to work with the contractor. The next day I confronted him with what I had found out, and told him we were still going to pay him what we had agreed upon.

A few days later I rode with him to pick up some shrubs for the backyard, and he shared with me what had happened to him. In just the last few days, his business partner had taken all the funds from their account and pled guilty on behalf of their company to fraud. Then his wife had told him that his children were not his and kicked him out of the house. He was living in his truck.

He told me that as a youth he had sung solos at the Crystal Cathedral in Garden Grove, California, but now when he turned his radio to Christian stations, as hard as he tried, he could not sing songs he had known so well. He thought, *Maybe God has deserted me, too.* But then, when I confronted him and told him we intended to work with him anyway, he left our home thinking, *Maybe God hasn't deserted me after all.*

A few days later he went to a church down the road from our home and for the first time trusted Christ as Savior. I was so glad that I had listened to and followed Jesus' command to bless those who despitefully use you. And I was so glad that I had drawn the family together to hear what Jesus said, and prayed that despite my anger I would be willing to do what Jesus told me to do.

I tell these stories, not because I was a great father, or even a good example. I simply want to point out that even in a busy world like ours, we can make family and family time a priority. And that as we live our lives together, God will provide opportunities for us to put His words into practice, and so to impress them on our children.

Your Situation Is Unique

I am fully aware that each family's situation is unique. Each of us faces different challenges, different strains. We live in a world that does not encourage the lifestyle described in Deuteronomy 6 and 11. We can see the almost imperceptible ways the god of this world is shaping society in order to overcome the good God intended when He gave us the gift of family.

Again, you and I are not called to enter culture wars that we cannot win. But each one of us is called to make the most of the gift of family. All of us are called to love God with our whole hearts, to live by His words and to impress God's words on the children on whom we have influence—not so much by formal teaching, but by the powerful impact of the informal as we let them see His words expressed in our lives.

Creating a Nurturing Climate

1. Give children unconditional love and acceptance.
2. Spend time with children in activities appropriate to their ages.

3. Spend time with each child individually.
4. Involve children in family discussions and decisions.
5. Consider participating in a homeschooling group.
6. Correct and discipline when necessary, explaining why.
7. Read aloud to the children and talk about questions that emerge.
8. Limit the number of organized sports the children participate in.
9. Encourage neighborhood playgroups. Playing football in our yard was big when our oldest was about ten.
10. Limit and supervise the use of computers, cell phones, Twitter, Facebook, etc.
11. Attend church as a family.
12. Develop family traditions: places we vacation, things we do.
13. As children grow older, encourage participation with adults in various activities.
14. Choose a family service project in which all can participate.
15. Explain your family's plan for giving, and encourage the children to participate.

7

The Gift of the Law

One of the most rewarding letters I have received from people who have read one of my books came from an older gentleman. He had purchased my *Encyclopedia of Bible Words*. He explained that as long as he remembered he had been anxious about God's Law and his responsibility to live up to the Commandments. Then he read the discussion of Law in my book. He said that he finally understood, and was now at peace.

I appreciated his letter. It is always a blessing to discover someone has been helped through your ministry. At the same time, I suspect his anxiety and uncertainty about the role of Law in the Christian's life are shared by many. Certainly those of us who have struggled to keep "the whole law" and yet have stumbled "at just one point" (James 2:10) can understand feelings of guilt and shame. At moments of personal failure, we hardly think of the Law as a gift. It seems so much more like a burden.

The truth is, Law is both a gift and a burden. In one sense biblical Law is the gift of a God who loves us deeply and yearns for us to experience the best in this life. In another sense, the Christian's freedom from the Law to live under grace releases us from a terrible burden. It is no wonder in the invisible war that Satan does all he can to create misunderstanding of the Law, and so overcome the good God intends with evil.

The Role of the Law in Sacred History

The Israelites lived in Egypt at first as aliens, then as slaves. They had heard stories of God's promise to their ancestor Abraham of a land of their own, but those promises were a dim memory. Aside from stories passed from generation to generation, the Israelites knew very little about the God of their forefathers.

Then, unexpectedly, Moses came out of the desert to announce that Abraham's God was about to perform miracles and win Israel's freedom. In the series of miracles that followed, Pharaoh, the ruler of what was then the most powerful nation on earth, was driven to his knees and the land of Egypt lay in ruins. The message to Israel was clear: God is powerful and loving, able to act in history on behalf of His people.

Then Moses led Israel out of Egypt, deep into the Sinai Peninsula. There, at Mount Sinai, God gave Israel His Law.

When we look at Old Testament Law we have to understand the historical situation. The people who followed Moses to freedom really did not know God. They had only recently seen His power and experienced His goodness. But they had no idea of His character, so different from that of the deities of Egypt and surrounding nations.

Now Israel had entered into a relationship with the living God, One who is not simply a power but a person. In this context, Law was intended first of all to reveal the kind of person God is, and second to teach Israel how to maintain a close personal relationship with Him. Should the people of Israel maintain that relationship by keeping the Law, great blessing would follow. In fact, the Law laid the foundation for a specially shaped society—one that enabled Israel to experience something of the coming eternal community of love.

Relationship with God in Law

The first question the freed slaves needed to answer was, What kind of person is this God who has called us into relationship? The enduring answer to that question was revealed to them in the Ten Commandments. Here we see a powerful reflection of God's nature and character.

The first four Commandments told Israel that God is unique. There is no other God, and He alone is to be worshiped. The next six Commandments unveiled for them the moral character of God and His values. God has, and He values, respect for individuals, for their rights and property. God has, and He values, loyalty and commitment in relationships. God guards, and He values, the lives and even the reputations of each individual. While God in His essential nature is far beyond our capacity to understand, He is also a person like us. And we learn about the kind of person He is through the Ten Commandments He gave to Israel.

The second question Israel needed to answer was, How do we live in intimate relationship with this person who has delivered us and has revealed Himself to us? The answer was that they were to be as much like Him as possible, again adopting and living by His values as expressed in the Ten Commandments.

After giving His people the Ten Commandments, God gave detailed instructions for a special way of life to Moses, who, in turn, taught the Israelites God's rules and ordinances. Moses' teachings, which were developed in the books of Exodus, Leviticus, Numbers and Deuteronomy, laid down a blueprint that God's Old Testament people were to follow in order to live in close relationship with God.

Perhaps the most striking and least understood aspect of Old Testament Law is that it laid out in detail the kind of society God yearned for His people to experience. In a society shaped by obedience to the Law, individuals would be secure and blessed. There would be no sexual abuse (see Leviticus 18). The rights and property of all would be protected (see Exodus 22). The poor would find help and at the same time maintain self-respect (see Leviticus 19:10; 23:22; 25:35–37; Deuteronomy 15:7–11). Anyone who committed a crime against a fellow Israelite would make restitution and be restored to a right relationship with God and his fellow citizens (see Exodus 22). Children would grow to adulthood in a healthy society, free from the fears and tensions that mar the lives of those in every other society.

The Choice

As we look through the Old Testament we are reminded again and again that God's Law was intended as a blessing for His people. But blessing could come only if Israel as a society followed the guidance God provided in His Law. Thus, the theme of choice is one we find over and over again in Scripture.

"Keep all my commandments always," God exhorted Israel, "*so that it might go well with* [*you*] and [your] children forever!" (Deuteronomy 5:29, emphasis added). Israel was called on "to observe the LORD's commands and decrees that I am giving you today *for your own good*" (10:13, emphasis added).

In the classic chapter on choice, Deuteronomy 28, Moses confronted Israel with the significance of the two opposing choices they could make: loyalty to God or going their own way. Moses began the chapter with the words, "If you fully obey the LORD your God and carefully follow all his commands," and then listed the blessings the nation could expect to experience. Then in mid-chapter Moses said, "However, if you do not obey the LORD your God and do not carefully follow all his commands," and went on to describe the national disasters that would follow national disobedience (Deuteronomy 28:15; see verses 16–68).

Both in giving the Law and in spelling out consequences of the choices Israel might make, God acted for the good of His people. Israel needed the guidance expressed in the Law, and also needed to understand the consequences of abandoning it.

No Salvation in the Law

Yet, even as Israel was enjoined to obey the Law of Moses, it did not follow that the people were "saved" by their obedience. The apostle Paul states this idea clearly: "No one will be declared righteous in [God's] sight by observing the law; rather, through the law we become conscious of sin" (Romans 3:20).

Paul teaches further that individual salvation is a matter of faith, not of works. No one in Old Testament times— or today—can earn a permanent relationship with God by following certain criteria. In Romans 4 Paul gives us the example of Abraham himself. God credited righteousness to Abraham on the sole basis of his trust in God's promise, just as today God welcomes to His family those who trust in Jesus. It has always been trust in God and in His promises that provides an individual with forgiveness of sin and a true personal relationship with Him.

So why did God give Israel the Ten Commandments and the extensive rules and regulations of the Mosaic Law? Remember that the Law was given to Israel as a nation. Israel's loyalty and obedience can be viewed as national characteristics; the blessings she would receive were national blessings. The Law provided the guidance Israel needed to build a society that would enable God's people to experience something of the fast approaching eternal community of love.

Satan's Strategy Exposed

Throughout sacred history, the Israelites had varying degrees of success in forming a society that embodied the lifestyle outlined in Moses' Law. And just as the Israelites' understanding of Law grew less relational and more pharisaical, so our own approach to Old Testament Law has become misguided. We have missed its true intent. Satan has a field day misleading us in relation to God's Law and, thus, overcoming good with evil.

The first tactic is to distort our concept of God. God gave the Law to reveal His moral character. Satan has convinced most of humankind that biblical Law casts God as a tyrant, eager to punish anyone who dares to violate one of His demands. One result of this is that many fear God and are driven away from Him.

In a sense it is unfortunate that Bible translators chose to render the Hebrew *torah* as "law." The essential meaning of *torah* is "teaching or instruction." In its biblical context, the Law was divine instruction on how Israel was to live close to the Lord, and experience His blessing. Law not only provided Israel with a clear revelation of God's moral character, but also guided Israel to fashion a society in which all would be blessed.

In our culture, "law" states what we must do, and is enforced by the coercive power of the state. It is not surprising, then, that when reading Old Testament "law," we assume that God demands our performance, and backs up His demand with His power to punish. With this distorted notion of biblical Law we humans might view God as a fearsome being, and when we fall short of the guidance provided in Scripture, we let guilt and shame drive us away from our Creator and Savior.

The second tactic, which follows closely, is to distort our concept of how we are made righteous before God. By promoting Old Testament Law as demand rather than guidance, Satan has led most people to assume that keeping the Law wins God's approval, and, thus, is the path to salvation.

Look once more at the apostle Paul's admonition: "No one will be declared righteous in [God's] sight by observing the law; rather, through the law we become conscious of sin." Every person who has ever lived is aware that in some respect he or she falls short of the way of life the Law describes. The intent of this knowledge that we cannot "perform" our way into salvation is that the sinner might turn away from self-effort, and trust entirely in God's love and forgiveness. The Law helps us understand that salvation is not found in a business transaction between a human and God. Salvation is found in a personal relationship with God entered into by faith in Jesus.

As we fall for Satan's scheme that promotes Law as a way of salvation, it follows that we also become blind to the Gospel. Some struggle to be "good enough," tormented by their failures and fears. Others simply abandon the struggle and substitute their own morality for the true morality God has revealed.

By distorting the concept of biblical Law, Satan has effectively overcome good with evil in far too many lives. He has distorted humankind's concept of God, producing fear of the One who loves each individual deeply. By casting Law as coercive demand rather than as guidance, Satan has induced guilt and shame, and has launched many on a quest for salvation rooted in self-effort rather than faith.

While this strategy has been most effective with nonbelievers, it has also had an impact on Christians. Far too many of us read the Bible from the perspective of Law rather than of grace. Far too many of us, when we fall short, doubt God's love rather than realizing that God, like any loving father whose two-year-old stumbles and falls, stoops to lift us up and set us on our feet again. Rather than feel uncertain about God's continuing love, we are to "approach the throne of grace with confidence, so that we may receive mercy [when we fall short] and find grace to help us in our time of need" (Hebrews 4:16).

Is the Law Relevant Today?

I have stressed the fact that the Law found in the Old Testament was a gift to the nation of Israel. God's Old Testament people were both a faith community and a nation; the Law provided the framework within which the nation could exist as a vital community of faith. For Israel, the Law provided both a revelation of the character of their God and a pattern for national life. As long as the nation followed the guidance provided by the Law, blessing would follow. But, God warned, if Israel as a nation abandoned the pattern of life portrayed by the Law, national disaster would surely follow. In this God was acting in grace to emphasize the importance of Israel's choices.

When we turn to the New Testament we find a totally different situation. There is no "Christian nation" in the sense that Israel was both nation and faith community. Instead, Christian communities are scattered groups of believers planted within essentially non-Christian cultures. While beliefs differ as to how much or how little these communities embody the ideals of Scripture, biblical Law addresses no individual or nation as it addressed Israel.

This raises an important question: What relevance does biblical Law have for individuals and for the Church? In describing the impact of our relationship with Jesus in his letter to the Romans, Paul gives us the answer: "Sin shall not be your master, because you are not under law, but under grace" (Romans 6:14). Israel was "under law," but Christians clearly are not. But this does not mean that the Law is now irrelevant.

This is true, first of all, because the Law of the Old Testament continues to reveal the character and values of God. When we read the Ten Commandments, we continue to see the face of God in them. When we read the Law, we continue to see a powerful reflection of God's nature and character.

In reading the Old Testament, or the New, it is important that we look deeply into the Word to see the God who spoke it. We Christians need to understand who this God is who has called us to Himself in Christ just as much as Israel needed to understand the God who delivered them from slavery in Egypt.

Second, Paul points out that the Law is still relevant because it is through the Law that we have knowledge of sin. That is, the Law serves as a standard against which we can evaluate our actions. When we use the Law this way, we see that we do not live up to the standard, and at times even consciously violate or rebel against it. If there were no standard established, we would not be able to tell that our actions are wrong and sinful. And if we did not know we were sinners, we would not realize that we need a Savior.

There is a third function of the Law for Christians today. We have seen that the Law provided divine guidance for the nation and people of Israel. It was given to point Israel to a way of life that would provide blessing for the nation, and enable its people to avoid evils. Today we Christians have a different source of divine guidance: the Holy Spirit who lives within us. In Paul's powerful exposition in Romans 8, he points out that we are to live "according to the Spirit" (verse 4) rather than follow the impulses of our sinful natures. One result of following the guidance provided by the Holy Spirit is that "the righteous requirements of the law" are "fully met in us" (verse 4).

Overcoming Evil with Good

Paul's teaching makes an important point. You and I are to focus on deepening our relationship with Jesus, aware that as we live close to Him the Holy Spirit will provide God's personal guidance as to the choices we are to make.

But how do we know when a choice we are contemplating is really from the Spirit rather than an expression of our own desires?

Paul's answer is that in following the Spirit's guidance, "the righteous requirements of the law" will be met. That is, if any action we take or contemplate taking violates the guidance given through the written Law, it cannot be an action prompted by the Spirit. God's Spirit does not contradict God's Word. What a valuable gift this function of the Law is for you and me today!

Approaching God's Law

1. Read the Old and New Testaments to come to know God better, to become aware of His values and commitments.

2. Let the Ten Commandments make you aware of sins you need to ask God's help to overcome.

3. Test decisions and choices you feel led to take against Scripture. The Holy Spirit will never lead you to violate God's written Word.

4. Do not assume you earn points with God by working hard to keep His Commandments. Stay close to Jesus and focus on responding as the Holy Spirit leads.

5. Do not take pride in being a "better Christian" than others. You do not know how far along they might be in their walks with Jesus.

6. Do not assume that the difficulties or suffering you experience indicates that God is punishing you for failure to keep His Law. Out of love God might use difficulties and suffering to discipline or train believers, with the intent of making us more Christlike.

7. Do not confuse personal convictions with God's standards. Be careful not to judge others in what Romans 14 calls "disputable matters."

8. Remember that God loves you no matter what. You might fall short, but God loves you for yourself, not for how well you perform.

8

The Gift of a
Community of Faith

Community is a persistent theme in this book, from the core community of marriage, to the family as a community, to God's plan in the Law to fashion Israel into a true community. And of course, casting its light on all these expressions of community is the eternal community of love that awaits us when Jesus returns, and history comes to an end.

We have already seen several characteristics of community. Community is marked by people in intimate and generally long-term relationships. Community is marked by shared values and loyalties. True community is marked by commitment and unconditional love. Ultimately, community is a safe haven, in which we can be real with others with the assurance that no matter what, we are loved. In a true community we can find support and encouragement to grow in our commitment to and love for the Lord. No wonder community is the setting within which we can experience some of the blessings that await us in God's eternal community of love.

The New and Better Way

The Law laid out a blueprint for the nation of Israel, which, if followed, would have provided community for the Israelites. But, as Old Testament history makes clear, this divinely given blueprint was never followed. Time and time again Israel fell into the ways of the surrounding heathen peoples. As God had forewarned, the choices made by the nation had devastating consequences. These choices made it impossible for God to provide the blessings He yearned to shower on His people.

Today, Paul tells us, we "are not under law, but under grace" (Romans 6:14). Paul does not in any way suggest by this that God no longer expects His children to live righteous and holy lives. The character of the God revealed in the Commandments has not changed. Nor has our calling as His people to reflect His character in all that we do. God simply has a new and better way of helping us grow in Christlikeness.

One of Paul's prayers for believers provides insight into that new and better way. Paul records his prayer in Ephesians 3:17–19:

> And I pray that you, being rooted and established in love, may have power, together with all the saints, to grasp how wide and long and high and deep is the love of Christ, and to know this love that surpasses knowledge—that you may be filled to the measure of all the fullness of God.

Note several things in this brief prayer. Paul asks that we be "rooted and established in love." There are several possibilities here, but the context makes it clear Paul is talking about our love for one another as believers. As Paul introduces his prayer he kneels before the Father, "from whom the whole family in heaven and on earth takes its name." Because God is our Father, we believers are an extended but very real family. As family members we are to be deeply rooted in love for one another. This love is vital if we, "together with all the saints," are to "be filled to the measure of all the fullness of God."

Just as God intended Israel to be a community of love as well as a nation, so God intends believers today to live as a community "rooted and established in love." It is not Law that will make this new community formed around Jesus a reflection of the eternal community of love. It is grace.

Love in Action

Love is hardly an unexpected theme here in the epistles. In the Last Supper with His disciples, the night before His crucifixion, Jesus gave His disciples a new command: "Love one another. As I have loved you, so you must love one another. All men will know that you are my disciples if you love one another" (John 13:34–35). This command is clear. Believers are to love one another, not just as neighbors, but as Jesus Himself loves, with selflessness and commitment that find expression in our daily lives.

We have many pictures in the epistles of how Christians should respond to Christ's words. In Romans 12, Paul wrote to new believers, reminding them that to fulfill Jesus' words, "love must be sincere." Members of the Christian community are to "hate what is evil; cling to what is good." They must "be devoted to one another in brotherly love" and "honor one another above yourselves." Within the context of this new Christian community, Paul told them "never [to] be lacking in zeal, but keep your spiritual fervor, serving the Lord. Be joyful in hope, patient in affliction, faithful in prayer. Share with God's people who are in need. Practice hospitality" (Romans 12:9–13).

We have an interesting if brief picture of a gathering of the early Church in 1 Corinthians 14:26: "When you come together, everyone has a hymn, or a word of instruction, a revelation, a tongue or an interpretation. All of these must be done for the strengthening of the church."

A passage in Colossians 3:16 gives us another picture of the same thing: "Let the word of Christ dwell in you richly as you teach and admonish one another with all wisdom, and as you sing psalms, hymns and spiritual songs with gratitude in your hearts to God."

These and similar passages give us a picture of what happened in the early Church when God's people got together to "teach and admonish" one another. And there is more—another portrait of those who gathered in the early Church. It is an "emotional" portrait of the family of God gathered in community.

> Therefore, as God's chosen people, holy and dearly loved, clothe yourselves with compassion, kindness, humility, gentleness and patience. Bear with each other and forgive whatever grievances you may have against one another. Forgive as the Lord forgave you. And over all these virtues put on love, which binds them all together in perfect unity. Let the peace of Christ rule in your hearts, since as members of one body you were called to peace.
>
> Colossians 3:12–15

"Church" Then and Now

If you have read the above thoughtfully, you have probably noticed something important. If these early Christians were "going to church," the church they were going to was significantly different from almost every church service we could imagine today.

For one thing, it seems that these meetings were highly participatory. The description "*everyone* has a hymn, or a word of instruction, a revelation, a tongue or an interpretation" just is not what happens in the church my wife and I attend Sunday mornings. Nor do we "teach and admonish one another with all wisdom." That seems to be the preacher's job, not ours.

But even the parts of church described here that we might consider to be "our" responsibility—meaning the personal relationships—do not match this picture of the early Church. The truth is, as I look around me Sunday morning I see mostly a congregation of strangers. I have no problem "bearing with" (putting up with) those I see. I hardly know the individual seated four persons away well enough to have grievances against him!

Now, the point of this is not to bash our church services. It is simply to point out that few churches are structured to encourage members to come to know and love each other deeply, or to enable all to exercise spiritual gifts actively. There is no doubt from Scripture or from Church history that believers in the early Church met in groups small enough for all to have a voice, and for everyone to know each other well.

For my wife and me today, Sunday church is important. But it is what happens on Monday evenings that is vital. On Monday evenings we gather at Allin and Barbara's house with twelve to fourteen other people. We share a meal, and catch up on what has been happening in each of our lives. Around the table we share our joys, our trials and our disappointments. Then we go into the living room and sit in a circle. In our particular group we look at the passage that was the basis for the pastor's message. We share our reactions, encouraging and at times exhorting each other. We close with prayer requests, and pray for each other. And then, usually, we simply stand around chatting. In the process, over time, we have come to know and to love each other deeply. And each of us has been ministered to, both by God's Word and by the words spoken in our gathering.

In a way it is not fair to compare our services today with communities of believers within the early Church. For at least three centuries of the Christian era there were no church buildings to go to. Believers met in homes in small gatherings. There they built intimate relationships. And there they ministered to each other, each using his or her gifts to build others up in the common faith. They were truly extended families, living together as and in communities. Undoubtedly, it was in and through these communities that Jesus' words were fulfilled: "By this all men will know that you are My disciples, if you love one another." And it was in and through these house churches that so many in that pagan world came to know Christ.

Satan's Strategy Exposed

Satan is committed to overcoming the good God intends through smaller family-like communities such as existed in the early Church and are reflected in Scripture. Satan understands the spiritual power that exists as believers grow in unity and love, joining together in prayer. Satan understands that spiritual gifts are designed to function in just the kinds of relationships that develop in such communities. And Satan understands that it is as we become invested in such communities that we may be "filled to the measure of all the fullness of God." One of Satan's major goals is to keep believers from participating in these life-transforming experiences.

The first tactic is to blind believers to their need for deeper Christian relationships than they find in going to church. Going to church on Sunday, or even participating in most Sunday school classes, is far from experiencing extended-family community as we have sketched it here. But Satan deceives us into believing that all the spiritual nurture we need is provided if we attend church faithfully on Sundays, sing hymns and listen to our pastors' sermons. The reality is that sitting in the pews on Sunday (or even singing in the choir) was never intended to replace the experience of true community within a smaller group of believers. It is in such smaller community groups, where we minister to and learn to love each other, that God's Spirit transforms us.

The second tactic is to convince believers that they are unlovable. "If others only knew what's inside of you," Satan's demons whisper, "no one would ever accept or love you." When we are overcome with guilt and shame, the idea of being in a group of believers where everyone is open and honest can be terrifying.

The third tactic is to disrupt relationships within such communities. Satan fosters gossip about things shared in the communities that should be held in confidence. He encourages misunderstandings and irritation with others. Paul implores the church to "bear with each other and forgive whatever grievances you may have against one another. Forgive as the Lord forgave you." Being committed to loving one another in the community group setting may be difficult. But it is essential, and Satan will do everything he can to erect walls between those of us who are now brothers and sisters.

The fourth tactic is to use the institutional aspects of the church to consume the time and efforts of those who are most committed. In a sense, the modern church is slightly schizophrenic. On the one hand, it exists to evangelize, promote worship and encourage spiritual growth. But, on the other hand, the modern church is also an institution, which requires upkeep. The property must be paid for and maintained. Boards and committees must meet. Programs for all ages must be organized and staffed.

In the typical church only a small percentage of the members are involved in these activities, and these few are viewed as the most "committed" of the congregation. But the very fact that they are so involved in the institution often means that they have little time left for those communities in which the real work of the church is done. And Satan sees to it that those who do focus on maintaining the institution are praised and are viewed as exemplary Christians.

Overcoming Evil with Good

The New Testament gives us three primary images for Christ's Church.

The first comes in Romans. Here Paul explains that we are part of the Body of Christ, and that "each member belongs to all the others" (Romans 12:5). Because we are so intimately linked to one another, we must use the gifts given by the Spirit to minister to each other. This analogy is developed in Corinthians when Paul stresses the importance of each person and what he or she contributes to the health and vitality of the whole (see 1 Corinthians 12).

The next image comes in Ephesians. In this letter, Paul emphasizes that we are family now, and that we take our identity as family from the fact that God is "the Father" (Ephesians 3:14). Ephesians also returns to the image of the body, affirming that there is "one body" (4:4) and that we should live lives worthy of this calling (see 4:1).

And third is the image of a holy temple—a "spiritual house"—constructed out of "living stones" (1 Peter 2:5). Peter teaches that the stones must be closely fitted each to the other to create a secure and enduring structure.

If we look carefully at the chapters where these images are developed we note two things. Each chapter emphasizes the spiritual bond that exists among believers. And each chapter contains a picture of how we are to love one another to maintain that bond.

In brief, each chapter implies—no, requires—that we Christians meet in smaller faith communities where we can experience what it means to be body, family and holy temple.

The gift of community is one of those wonderful gifts that God gives to His Church. And in the invisible war, Satan is intent on overcoming with evil the good that God wants us to experience in a community of faith.

Growth and Change

The first time I experienced community was in the navy in 1953. I had made a conscious commitment to Jesus, and had begun to study my Bible intently. About four months after my experience with the Lord, I started a Bible study on my base, the New York Port of Embarcation in Brooklyn. Every noon I went to the base chapel, where in time I was joined by three others. These were a soldier, Larabee, and two civilians who worked on the base, Lee and Conrad. And myself. There was only one unusual thing about our tiny group: Lee never said a word. For months she came, but remained utterly silent.

During her silent months in our Bible study, Lee listened to the three of us share and pray. None of us ever pressured her, simply accepting her as she was. Finally, she spoke a few words. Gradually she participated more. As she began to feel safe with us, she told us more of her story. Lee had come to know Christ as a single mother with one daughter, and had joined a church. But somehow the church never seemed to bring her closer to Jesus. She was eager to learn, but her life remained empty. Quiet and shy in our little foursome, Lee remained reserved in the office where she worked and at church, where she would find an isolated place on a pew and sit alone.

When I was discharged from the navy in the spring of 1955, our little community broke up. It was several years later that I returned to New York City, where I had been stationed most of my navy career. One of the first things I did was to telephone Lee. I was invited to her home in Bay Ridge one evening, and was surprised to walk into a room full of people. As Lee introduced me to her guests, she explained about the gathering.

Some time before, a Billy Graham crusade had come to the city. Because of the confidence she had gained in our little community in the navy chapel, Lee had actually begun witnessing to others about her faith. When the crusade came to town, she invited everyone she knew, including co-workers, to go with her. And all of the nineteen people in her living room that evening had committed their lives to Jesus at the crusade because Lee had reached out to them.

That is what is so amazing about little communities of faith where we can come to know, to love and to pray for each other. They are one of God's most wonderfully good gifts. They are soil in which the Holy Spirit works true transformation.

Experiencing a Community of Faith

1. Encourage the leadership of your church to promote small groups and to provide training for those who participate.
2. Gather a few friends who will commit to meeting together weekly to share, pray, study and encourage each other.
3. If most people seem unwilling to respond to your initiative, look for just one or two who will meet with you.
4. Establish ground rules. Here are a few important examples: Everything spoken in the group will be kept confidential; each member will share only as much of a private nature as he or she is comfortable doing; you will pray for each other daily.
5. Look for opportunities to strengthen relationships by making contact during the week or doing things together.
6. Commit to caring for each other as you come to know each other better.
7. Be open and honest about your thoughts and feelings. Put aside fear of confronting one another in loving ways.
8. Invite others to join your community group.
9. Take time for each person who wants to do so to tell his or her story. At times, and especially as others join your group, have members retell their stories.

9

The Gift of Restoration

We call them the "old" and the "new" testaments. There are reasons for this distinction. Long ago Jeremiah predicted that God would one day make a "new covenant" with His people. The new covenant would replace the Law covenant introduced at Sinai. Even though the Old Testament tells the story of the old covenant, and the New Testament unveils the wonders of the new, the two testaments constitute one revelation by the Creator of His purposes and promises. One of these purposes is ultimately to create an eternal community of love, a theme first glimpsed in Genesis 1. Intimately linked to this ultimate purpose is a revelation of good gifts intended to enable us to experience some of the benefits of the eternal community in our own time.

After Satan's overwhelming defeat in the initial rebellion, the devil and his demons have been committed to overcoming good with evil, twisting the gifts of God to cause suffering rather than blessing. As God's people, our mission is to overcome the evil with good, enabling us to experience the blessings the Lord yearns for us to know. Perhaps one of the most surprising but important gifts to the believing community of the Old Testament and the believing community of the New is the gift of restoration.

God Teaches Restoration

If we note the flow of the Pentateuch, the first five books of the Bible, we discover a fascinating sequence of events. God made covenant promises to Abraham and his descendants. When they were enslaved and helpless in Egypt, God intervened to redeem, claiming the Israelites as His own people. Moses then led the reclaimed people to Mount Sinai, where God gave Israel a Law that revealed His character and His expectations for His people. That Law also laid out a blueprint for a society in which Israel could experience some of the blessings of the eternal community of love.

But the Israelites turned their backs rebelliously on the Lord. They constructed a golden calf to be their god. Immediately following in the text of Exodus, we find instructions for a worship center, for the ordination of priests and for a sacrificial system. The details of the sacrificial system are developed in Leviticus, along with further instruction on how Israel was to show that they are a unique people, dedicated to God. The sequence ends with a list of holy days and festivals the people were to observe, celebrating their relationship with the One God.

As we analyze this sequence we see a pattern. Redemption was followed by instruction on how to live in close relationship with the Redeemer. But almost immediately the people sinned. Yet the sin did not lead to rejection by God. Instead a priesthood and sacrifices for sins were instituted, sacrifices that would restore the violated relationship. A worship center was established where the restored people could come to meet with God. And then a series of festivals was outlined, where the redeemed and restored people could celebrate in God's presence.

When we follow this development through the books of Moses, we begin to sense the importance of restoration in the life of the believing community.

Justice Systems, Old and New

The nature of the gift of restoration is seen clearly when we compare features of modern justice systems with those of the justice system God designed for the community of Israel. Take the case of theft, a common but not a violent crime. In our modern justice systems the act of stealing is viewed as a crime against the state where the theft was committed. The response to such a crime is to find, convict and punish the perpetrator. If convicted, the criminal is sentenced to prison for an appropriate length of time. When the sentence is completed, even though he has "paid his debt to society," an ex-convict is likely to have difficulty finding a job and being reintegrated into society. In this process the victim of the crime is usually forgotten. The victim may be called on to testify at the trial, but there is no repayment of the loss he or she suffered.

In the justice system designed by God for Israel, the crime is viewed as an offense against the victim, not against the state. And the goal is not to punish. The goal of the Old Testament justice system is both to make the victim whole, and to reintegrate the perpetrator into the community. Leviticus 6 makes the process of restoration clear.

> "If anyone sins and is unfaithful to the LORD by deceiving his neighbor about something entrusted to him or left in his care or stolen, or if he cheats him, or if he finds lost property and lies about it, or if he swears falsely, or if he commits any such sin that people may do—when he thus sins and becomes guilty, he must return what he has stolen. . . . He must make restitution in full, add a fifth of the value to it and give it all to the owner on the day he presents his guilt offering. And as a penalty he must bring to the priest, that is, to the LORD, his guilt offering. . . . In this way the priest will make atonement for him before the LORD, and he will be forgiven for any of these things he did that made him guilty."
>
> Leviticus 6:1–7

In cases of violence involving injury, the modern justice system punishes the criminal and leaves the victim to suffer his losses. In the system designed for Israel, the goal is still to make the victim whole. The principle of an eye for an eye or a tooth for a tooth governs, with the intent of restraining individuals from purposely harming others (see Exodus 21:24; Deuteronomy 19:21). It is also clear in this that neither the injured person nor a relative is allowed to take vengeance by causing even greater injury to the perpetrator. In practice, it is likely that a monetary value for the lost faculty was set or negotiated, and the victim was compensated for his loss (compare Exodus 21:18–19).

In this system, the perpetrator is identified, makes restoration for any loss suffered by the victim and acknowledges his act publicly by bringing a guilt offering to the Lord. This identifies the crime as both an offense against the victim and a sin against God. With the victim compensated and the sin publicly confessed through the guilt offering, the perpetrator is restored to his or her place within the Old Testament faith community.

A New Testament Example

As we have noted, the Church does not exist as a "Christian nation," but rather as numerous faith communities. Just as there are today Jewish communities in various nations, so Christian communities are scattered throughout the world. The nations within which Christian communities exist may be favorable to the faith, neutral or actively hostile. But today as with ancient Israel, believers will, in Moses' words, commit "such sin that people may do." When this happens we Christians are to model our response after the pattern set in Scripture.

A classic example of handling sin in a godly manner, allowing for restoration, is seen in the Corinthian church. This episode is mentioned throughout Paul's letters to that congregation. In 1 Corinthians 5:1, Paul outlined the situation: A man "has his father's wife," an obvious case of egregious sexual immorality. The sin, which should have "filled you with grief," was instead ignored by the congregation. Incensed, Paul demanded that they put the man who was doing this "out of your fellowship."

The church responded and the man was expelled. But Paul picked up the story in 2 Corinthians 2:5–11. It seems that "the punishment inflicted on him by the majority" had its intended result. The man abandoned the sinful relationship. But that was not enough for some who apparently were slow to embrace reconciliation. Paul had to write the church again, to encourage them "to forgive and comfort him, so that he will not be overwhelmed by excessive sorrow. I urge you, therefore, to reaffirm your love for him." Strikingly, Paul added that this response was "in order that Satan might not outwit us. For we are not unaware of his schemes."

Paul was affirming to the New Testament Church that, just as in the faith community of old, any violation of rights or persons must be addressed. And he was affirming, equally, that the goal after an individual repudiates the sin is to restore him or her to full fellowship within the community.

Additional teaching in 1 Corinthians 6 reflects clearly the principles expressed in the older testament. Here the issue is cheating and doing wrong to a fellow Christian. Some who were victims took their cases to pagan law courts, something Paul viewed as shameful. Paul called for the Church to appoint judges from among the congregation to evaluate and settle such disputes.

Again, the goal of intervention by the Church is not to punish, but to make the victim whole, and to restore the perpetrator's relationship with God and with his or her brothers and sisters. To settle for anything less hands Satan a victory.

Satan's Strategy Exposed

One of the apostle Paul's most heartfelt exhortations is found in Philippians:

> If you have any encouragement from being united with Christ, if any comfort from his love, if any fellowship with the Spirit, if any tenderness and compassion, then make my joy complete by being like-minded, having the same love, being one in spirit and purpose.
>
> Philippians 2:1–2

How vital it is that in the faith communities scattered across the globe we Christians maintain our unity in love. It is only through love for one another, as Paul points out in Ephesians 3:17–19, that we are enabled to "be filled to the measure of all the fullness of God." It is no wonder, then, that one of Satan's strategies is to shatter the unity of believing communities, and prevent any kind of reconciliation that would enable us to experience some of the blessings that will be found in the eternal community of love at history's end.

Satan uses many tactics in carrying out this strategy, tactics that are used against the guilty and tactics that are used against the community of which the guilty individual has been a part.

Tactics Used to Destroy the Guilty

In the book of Romans, Paul argues that people know right from wrong. When we do what we know is wrong, our consciences "[bear] witness" (Romans 2:15). The result is usually one of two reactions: We either accuse ourselves or excuse ourselves. Satan recognizes these two responses, and actively supports both.

The first tactic is to increase the accusation. Satan and his demons are quick to whisper their lies into our minds any time we feel guilt and shame about a transgression. "You're hopeless," they hiss. "You're nothing but a failure, and the next time you're tempted, you'll fail again. There's no use trying to overcome that habitual sin. God can't really love you. You don't deserve His love, and you never will. Give up."

And once we accept those lies about ourselves, we open the door for lies about our relationships with others: "You don't dare let others know you. If they knew what you are really like, they'd hate you. Or feel contempt toward you. They would never again want to have anything to do with you. No, you've got to keep your real feelings, your fears and your failures buried. Get out there and pretend to be one of those 'victorious' Christians who've gotten it all together and who never fall into sin."

This tactic of magnifying guilt and shame has proven successful over the centuries, and Satan turns to it frequently.

The second tactic is to shift the blame. Sometimes we respond to wrong we have done by excusing ourselves. Down deep we know we are responsible, but we shift the blame. We saw earlier an example of the drive to excuse ourselves and our actions in the story of the Fall. Adam blamed Eve for his choice to eat the forbidden fruit; Eve blamed the serpent for deceiving her. Adam even suggested that God was at fault because God gave Eve to him!

We do not like to think that we are fully responsible for the choices we make. And Satan has a host of excuses to help us along in that thinking: "Your parents didn't love you. You were just born that way. Everyone else does it, too." And so on. Satan is more than eager to help us think of excuses and of ways to shift blame to others.

Tactics Used to Disrupt Community

A cursory look at the situation in Corinth in which a man "has his father's wife" exposes Satan's tactics against communities of faith.

The first tactic is to encourage the community to overlook obvious sin. The fact that Satan was successful in keeping the church at Corinth from dealing with the man who was having sexual relations with his father's wife outraged Paul.

What the community should have done was to be "filled with grief" and put the man out of their fellowship. The man's action was affecting not only himself but the whole fellowship, including the potential for that fellowship to become a truly transforming community.

The second tactic is to cause overreaction. Satan encourages within the fellowship the natural feeling that a guilty person should be punished. And all too often, we Christians feel that it is up to us to make sure the person *is* punished.

As we saw from Paul's second letter to the Corinthians, the church responded to Paul's exhortation. They confronted the man, and put him out of the church. As a result the man faced his sin, confessed it and broke off the illicit relationship. After the man repented, however, the Christians refused to restore him to a place within their fellowship. Having condemned the man, they now excluded him. The man was apparently suffering "excessive sorrow" at this response from the Christian community.

Paul considered the continuing condemnation by the fellowship of a repentant brother to be a "scheme of Satan." What the church needed to do was to "forgive and comfort him." Paul urged these Christians "to reaffirm [their] love for him."

Overcoming Evil with Good

Paul was aware of the struggles believers face, and expressed his confidence that those who fall short can restore and be restored. Paul told the Corinthians that, despite disappointments, "we do not lose heart" (2 Corinthians 4:16). He explained, "We fix our eyes not on what is seen, but on what is unseen. For what is seen is temporary, but what is unseen is eternal" (verse 18).

In Christ, not only is there the *possibility* of change for those who fall, but there is the *certainty* of change. Paul was "convinced that one died for all, and therefore all died. And he died for all, that those who live should no longer live for themselves but for him who died for them and was raised again" (2 Corinthians 5:14–15). To Paul it was impossible that this purpose for which Christ died would go unfulfilled. We Christians, who have been given life in Christ, will reach the place where we no longer live for ourselves, but for Him.

Paul's conclusion for the Church is simple: "From now on we regard no one from a worldly point of view." We no longer base our evaluations on what we can see in a person's life or character. We know that "if anyone is in Christ, he is a new creation; the old has gone, the new has come!" Our role in the lives of our brothers and sisters is a ministry of reconciliation—of helping them become in fact who they are in Christ. Christ committed to us the ministry of reconciliation, a ministry based on God's own great reconciling act in Christ, when He died for us, "not counting men's sins against them" (2 Corinthians 5:16–19).

Satan understands the transforming power of Jesus' love for us and of our love for Him. Satan's tactics are designed to blind us to the transforming power of forgiveness and restoration.

Not That This Is Easy

We tend to think of restoration as a principle that applies solely to Christian communities, but there is also a very important personal application.

Some years ago I was speaking at a pastors' conference at the Lake Hume conference grounds in Northern California. During the week a number of pastors and youth ministers asked to speak with me privately. Each had a question that I soon realized revolved around a common theme. The youth ministers told me about God's blessing on their teens, but each of the leaders felt lack of support and interest on the part of their churches' pastors. The pastors told similarly about God's blessing on their churches, but each talked about strained relationships with one or more members of the church board. Without exception, despite evident blessings on their ministries, the youth pastors and ministers wondered if the interpersonal conflicts that so disturbed them were a sign from God that they should move on.

What did I think they should do?

I responded to each group with two brief instructions given by Jesus. The first was: "If you are offering your gift at the altar and there remember that your brother has something against you, leave your gift there in front of the altar. First go and be reconciled to your brother; then come and offer your gift" (Matthew 5:23). The second was: "If your brother sins against you, go and show him his fault, just between the two of you" (Matthew 18:15).

The message is clear, I said. Whoever might be at fault in the strained relationship, whether it is you or your brother, it is your responsibility to go to him to seek restoration of the relationship.

In each case the pastor or youth minister essentially replied with these words: "But that's hard."

Yes, it is hard to maintain unity in the Christian community. And Satan will do all he can to use our sins, our faults and our failures to drive wedges between us and other believers. But we are called to be one Body, one family, one holy temple in the Lord. And God has given us the gift of restoration so that we might overcome Satan's evil with good.

Actively Seeking Restoration

1. Do not ignore sin in your congregation or in a Christian friend. Be willing to speak the truth in love when a brother or sister falls into sin.
2. Affirm your love for and support of those who are ready to confess and repudiate their sins.
3. Be quick to recognize your own sins and weaknesses. Be willing to ask forgiveness if you have hurt others and be willing to go to others who have hurt you, with a view to restoration of your relationship.
4. Refrain from condemning or looking down on others who have fallen. Remember that restoration requires "not counting [their] sins against them" (2 Corinthians 5:19).
5. Do not become discouraged by what you see in others. If Christ is in their hearts, they *will* change.
6. The greatest witness we can give to the presence of Christ in our lives does not come by taking pains to "look good"; the greatest witness we can give to Jesus is the changes others see in our lives when we are open and honest—with ourselves and with them (see 2 Corinthians 3:18).

10

The Gift of God's Discipline

What does it mean that God disciplines us as His children? For one thing it means God has as much love for us as we do for our own families. Perhaps more importantly, it means that as a loving parent corrects and disciplines his or her own brood, so God is committed to correct and discipline us. And for a wonderful purpose. But what does it mean for God to discipline us?

If we look at the Bible's book of Proverbs as a model of childrearing, most of us find the familiar depictions about discipline to be a bit harsh. Is this how God views His relationship toward us—by not "sparing" the rod?

"Folly [a stubborn penchant for doing wrong] is bound up in the heart of a child," one proverb claims, "but the rod of discipline will drive it far from him" (Proverb 22:15). The case for using the rod is stated even more strongly in Proverbs 23:13–14. There the writer advises: "Do not withhold discipline from a child; if you punish him with the rod, he will not die. Punish him with the rod and save his soul from death." Another proverb states: "He who spares the rod hates his son, but he who loves him is careful to discipline him" (Proverb 13:24).

Now, it is true that the book of Proverbs does not present itself as rules or promises. Rather, Proverbs records general principles for living in harmony with others that were developed over the centuries by God's people. In a sense we could call Proverbs a handbook on living in community. The proverbs suggest what contributes to building the kind of community God outlines in the Law, and describe what hinders. Still, it is not surprising that when our eyes fall on these words about using "the rod" on children (a supple switch, by the way, not a club!), many of us tend to look away.

A Case for "Grace"?

An alternative view of the gift of discipline is given in Exodus 15–17, which describes the Israelites' journey from Egypt to Mount Sinai. The Israelites witnessed the devastating plagues God sent on Egypt to win their freedom. They knelt in terror as Pharaoh's chariot army pursued them to the edge of the sea, which miraculously opened to let them pass and then crashed over the Egyptian forces. Leaving the site of this final triumph over their slave masters, they joined Miriam, Moses' sister, in a song of triumph.

Just three days later they panicked when the only water they could find was bitter and undrinkable. God turned it sweet and drinkable. Then some twelve days later the whole crowd turned on Moses, longing for the food they had eaten in Egypt and accusing Moses of plotting to kill them. God provided miraculously a great flock of quail and manna, crispy, honey-flavored wafers that appeared with the morning dew. As the Israelites traveled on they reached a barren, waterless tract. Now the people were almost ready to kill Moses. But God used Moses to produce a stream of water from a rock.

On the entire trip from Egypt to Sinai, God overlooked the people's disobedience, their lack of faith and their constant hostility toward Moses. At each stage of the journey God simply provided what they thought they needed. Some might call this "grace." But the more of this kind of grace the people received, the less they respected or responded to the Lord. Then while Moses was meeting with God atop Mount Sinai, the people asked Aaron to shape a calf figure out of gold, bowed down to it and claimed that the idol was the god who had brought them out of Egypt.

The Rest of the Story

At Mount Sinai the people were given a Law, spelling out what God expected from them. A year later Moses led the Israelites away from Sinai toward the land God had promised to Abraham, Isaac and Jacob. On the way, the experiences of the journey to Sinai were repeated . . . with a significant difference. We read about it in Numbers 11–14. Now when the people complained, fire from the Lord consumed some on the outskirts of the camp. When the people wailed that they had lost their appetite for manna and demanded meat, God provided enough quail to feed the people for a month . . . and struck the people with a plague.

Approaching the borders of Canaan the people were frightened by reports of the size and power of the Canaanites. They refused to respond when God told them to enter the land, and decided it would "be better for us to go back to Egypt" (Numbers 14:3). Moses led them back into the wilderness, where over a span of some 38 years, everyone over the age of twenty died.

There is one verse that effectively contrasts the impact of the parallel events described in Exodus 15–17 and Numbers 11–14. After four decades had passed, Moses was able to say to the new generation of Israelites, "All of you who held fast to the LORD your God are still alive today" (Deuteronomy 4:4).

Grace without discipline was hardly grace at all. It was grace in the form of discipline that fashioned the second generation of freed Israelites into a responsive community, ready to inherit the blessings God had promised.

Choice and Discipline

Earlier in this book we looked at our God-given gift of choice. That gift is reemphasized as we look at God's gift of discipline. Deuteronomy 28 lays out clearly the choices facing Israel throughout its history. The community of Israel can remain loyal to the Lord and committed to obeying Him. Or the community of Israel can turn its back on the Lord, go after other gods and ignore God's commandments. The first choice leads to great blessing (see verses 1–13). The second choice leads to terrible disaster (see verses 15–68).

The prophets saw this passage as a key to interpreting events in Israel's history. Thus, Amos looked at events in his own time through the lens of Deuteronomy 28 and, speaking for God, complained that Israel had failed to respond to God's discipline:

> "I gave you empty stomachs in every city and lack of bread in every town, yet you have not returned to me," declares the LORD. . . . "Many times I struck your gardens and vineyards, I struck them with blight and mildew. Locusts devoured your fig and olive trees, yet you have not returned to me," declares the LORD.
>
> Amos 4:6, 9

The discipline of disaster was never a raw display of divine anger, but rather a call to the community to come back to its roots in a loyal and obedient relationship with the Lord.

Satan's Strategy Exposed

Satan is fully aware of both the nature of God's discipline and ancient Israel's failure to respond. Satan does all he can to disguise the truth that discipline is an expression of grace and that Israel's failure to respond kept the community from being blessed. Today, in the invisible war, Satan uses passages like those we have looked at to distort our view of God and sow confusion. He plants the idea that there is a God of the Old Testament who is harsh and mean without cause, and a God of the New Testament who would not think of permitting anyone to suffer. He does all he can to suppress the truth that God's discipline is an expression of love and grace.

The first tactic is to make sure we see discipline strictly as punishment. In fact, the basic meaning of *discipline* is "instruction and correction." Most parents realize that their children need each aspect of discipline—instruction, correction and sometimes punishment—to help them grow up as healthy, self-controlled adults who can have healthy relationships with others and with God. To see discipline solely as punishment distorts the biblical concept.

The second tactic is to convince us that God is both capricious and easily angered. If we do anything He considers to be wrong, He will make sure we suffer for it. In portraying God as an angry person, Satan tries to make sure that we never respond to Scripture's invitation to "come boldly to the throne of grace" in order to receive mercy for our sins and "grace to help" us avoid them next time. If Satan can use this distorted image of an angry God to make us doubt God's love, then Satan will keep us from that comfortable confidence in God's love that frees us to experience His presence.

The third tactic is to attempt to convince us that whenever something painful happens to us, God is punishing us. And terrible things do happen to us. We lose our jobs, loved ones die, we contract cancer, our life savings are taken by an identity thief, a child is crippled in an accident. Satan whispers, "It must be your fault," and we wonder what awful thing we could have done to deserve such suffering. Then Satan smirks as we go over the list of things we should have done—prayed more, read the Bible more intently, not skipped church so often. It is even more painful for truly faithful Christians who have done all God asks and more, and simply cannot find out what the sin was that caused all this pain.

The idea that God is punishing us whenever something goes wrong in our lives is one of Satan's most effective lies. In no case does Satan want us to understand the true nature of discipline, or the purposes that God can achieve through our suffering.

Overcoming Evil with Good

Back in Proverbs we might be disturbed at the picture of a child being struck with a "rod." But one thing is clear. The parent in these verses is not striking out in anger. He or she is acting in love, deeply concerned that the child learn to make the right choices in life and thus to "save his soul from death." It is a parent's duty to help a child develop boundaries and to learn the standards by which he will live as a member of his community. According to Dr. Hansa D. Bhargava, a specialist in pediatrics, permissive childrearing with no routines or limits produces kids "who have no rules, no curfews, no dress code, and no manners." And it produces children without self-discipline who rebel against authority and are unable to become contributing parts of a closely knit community.

The compilers of Proverbs understood the contrast in the two phases of Israel's journey to the Promised Land: the permissiveness exhibited in the first phase of the journey, and the discipline exercised in the second phase of the journey. Only a people who had experienced training, correction and, yes, punishment would be responsive to the Lord and ultimately experience the blessings He yearned to pour out on them.

All in the Family

Generally we learn about the gift of discipline in the context of the family. This is the case in Proverbs. It is the case with Amos, where the faith community itself is encouraged to be an extended family. And family is emphasized in the Bible's key passage on discipline, Hebrews 12. Here the writer addresses what he calls a "word of encouragement" to those whom God addresses as "sons": "My son, do not make light of the Lord's discipline, and do not lose heart when he rebukes you, because the Lord disciplines those he loves, and he punishes everyone he accepts as a son" (Hebrews 12:5–6).

The writer continues: "Endure hardship as discipline; God is treating you as sons. . . . Our fathers disciplined us for a little while as they thought best; but God disciplines us for our good, that we may share in his holiness" (verses 7, 10).

This does not mean that divine discipline seems pleasant at the time. But God's promise is that later on "it produces a harvest of righteousness and peace for those who have been trained by it" (verse 11).

A man in the Bible named Asaph struggled with this concept—the "unpleasantness" of being treated by God as a son or daughter.

Asaph was a music leader in the Temple that was designed by David and constructed by Solomon. But Asaph was becoming a bitter man. He confessed, "I envied the arrogant when I saw the prosperity of the wicked" (Psalm 73:3). It seemed to Asaph that the wicked in Israel were wealthy and healthy, "free from the burdens common to man" (verse 5). Asaph was also aware of the character of those who "had everything." They were proud and callous, scoffers who were filled with malice, men who clothed themselves in violence. Bitterly Asaph concluded, "This is what the wicked are like— always carefree, they increase in wealth" (verse 12).

What ate at Asaph was that he had none of the seeming blessings that the wicked possessed. Asaph could not help feeling that "surely in vain have I kept my heart pure; in vain have I washed my hands in innocence. All day long I have been plagued; I have been punished every morning" (verses 13–14).

Asaph's feelings of being treated unfairly by God ran deep. But he was a worship leader at the Temple. To share his feelings, Asaph decided, would be to betray God's children (see verse 15). Yet the more Asaph struggled to understand, the more oppressive the situation seemed. "Why them, Lord?" and "Why me?" were the cries of Asaph's heart.

Then one day, as Asaph was entering the sanctuary of God, it all came together. "Then," he wrote, "I understood their final destiny" (verse 17). The apparently blessed life of those who reject God's discipline has placed them on "slippery ground." They feel no need of God, and so He has no place in their lives. In the end God will "cast them down to ruin" (verse 18).

At this realization, Asaph saw his complaint as senseless and ignorant. Asaph lived in the presence of a God who was always with him, a God who held his hand and provided counsel. A God who afterward "will take me into glory" (verse 24).

Realizing that despite his trials and his troubles God was with him, Asaph concluded, "As for me, it is good to be near God" (verse 28).

We see the correlation between the experience of the Israelites on their journey toward Canaan and the experience of Asaph centuries later. In each case there are people who seem to be able to sidestep the cares of this world, and there are people who experience hardship. Of the two groups, those who face hardship and are disciplined by it find a deeper, more committed relationship with the Lord, one that "produces a harvest of righteousness and peace for those who have been trained by it."

Last Words on Discipline

Godly discipline is an important theme throughout Scripture. Here are a few passages that help us embrace what it means to be part of God's family.

From Paul:

Therefore, since we have been justified through faith, we have peace with God through our Lord Jesus Christ, through whom we have gained access by faith into this grace in which we now stand. And we rejoice in the hope of the glory of God. Not only so, but we also rejoice in our sufferings, because we know that suffering produces perseverance; perseverance, character; and character, hope. And God does not disappoint us, because God has poured out his love into our hearts by the Holy Spirit, whom he has given us.

Romans 5:1–5

From Peter:

Now for a little while you may have had to suffer grief in all kinds of trials. These have come so that your faith—of greater worth than gold, which perishes even though refined by fire—may be proved genuine and may result in praise, glory and honor when Jesus Christ is revealed.

1 Peter 1:6–7

Dear friends, do not be surprised at the painful trial you are suffering, as though something strange were happening to you. . . . Those who suffer according to God's will should commit themselves to their faithful Creator and continue to do good.

1 Peter 4:12, 19

It is the writer of the book of Hebrews who has the last word for us on the subject: "Endure hardship as discipline; God is treating you as sons." The writer goes on:

For what son is not disciplined by his father? If you are not disciplined (and everyone undergoes discipline), then you are illegitimate children and not true sons. Moreover, we have all had human fathers who disciplined us and we respected them for it. How much more should we submit to the Father of our spirits and live! Our fathers disciplined us for a little while as they thought best; but God disciplines us for our good, that we may share in his holiness. No discipline seems pleasant at the time, but painful. Later on, however, it produces a harvest of righteousness and peace for those who have been trained by it. Therefore, strengthen your feeble arms and weak knees. "Make level paths for your feet," so that the lame may not be disabled, but rather healed.

Hebrews 12:8–13

Responding to Divine Discipline

1. Never jump to the conclusion that painful experiences are always punishment inflicted by an angry God.

2. Hold fast to the conviction that what is happening is filtered through God's love.

3. If you are aware of any sins in your life that God might be dealing with, confess and repudiate them.

4. See painful expediencies primarily as discipline designed to mature God's children and enable you to share in God's holiness.

5. Do not give up under the pressure of pain or suffering, but commit yourself to God and "continue to do good."

6. Meditate on Hebrews 5:8: "Although [Jesus] was a son, he learned obedience from what he suffered."

7. Thank God for every experience, even the most difficult, and praise Him for His wisdom and love.

=11=

The Gift of Uniqueness

The truth expressed in Psalm 139:13–16 is an uncomfortable one for many people. In these verses David celebrated God's role in making him the unique individual that he was.

> For you created my inmost being; you knit me together in my mother's womb. I praise you because I am fearfully and wonderfully made; your works are wonderful, I know that full well. My frame was not hidden from you when I was made in the secret place. When I was woven together in the depths of the earth, your eyes saw my unformed body. All the days ordained for me were written in your book before one of them came to be.

The implication is that God was personally involved in shaping David to be the person he became. The genes that governed David's development were placed carefully along chromosomes, and the result was the unique individual we know as Israel's greatest king.

Now, maybe David was not as tall as Saul. But he was quite handsome. And David proved to be strong and charismatic. God shaped the perfect man for the job God had in mind when "all the days ordained" for David were written in God's book.

The further implication is that God is involved personally in shaping us into the unique individuals we become. It is an implication that can be troubling.

My Nose! I Hate My Nose!

Talk to most any teenage girl and the notion that God could have had anything to do with her nose is repugnant. *If God loved me, how could He have given me such a big nose?*

Of course, the nose probably is not really oversized. But if it is not the nose, it is the mousy color of her hair, or the feet she cannot squeeze into a size 7 shoe. In time as she matures, these "defects" will not seem great. But some girls will carry the feeling that they are unattractive into adulthood.

There are more serious questions we could raise about the idea that our uniqueness is a gift from God. It is all right to claim this for the person with the high IQ, or the person whose athletic ability makes him a highly paid professional. But what about the individual who hovers around average, or a person like my daughter, Joy, who was brain-damaged at birth and will spend her life at the intellectual level of a five-year-old?

And how about all those plain girls who live in a society that glorifies beauty and sexual appeal? And how about those men who are not gifted and who struggle just to make a living? When we examine the notion that each individual is unique, and that our uniqueness is a gift of God, we cannot help wondering if God is really being fair. And we cannot help realizing that the range of differences in people and in their lives gives Satan another opportunity to seek to overcome good with evil.

Satan's Strategy Exposed

Satan uses the uniqueness of individuals in a variety of ways to promote evil. Here are some of his tactics: He encourages envy and jealousy; he promotes hostility; he seeks to make us dissatisfied with our lot; he attacks our sense of self-worth; he stimulates covetousness and strife. If we are to experience now some of the blessings to be ours in the eternal community of love, we need to recognize and counter Satan's plan to use our uniqueness for evil.

Satan's tactics are seen in stories throughout Scripture. In Genesis 29 we read about Jacob, Rachel and Leah. The text tells us that Leah had "weak eyes" but "Rachel was lovely in form, and beautiful" (Genesis 29:17). Each of the women ended up married to Jacob, but the pain Leah experienced is summed up in the names of the first two sons she bore: *Reuben*, "for the LORD has seen my misery," and *Simeon*, "because the LORD heard that I am not loved" (verses 32–33). Rachel, who was childless for many years, was jealous of her sister and complained to Jacob, "Give me children, or I'll die!" (Genesis 30:1). Each compared her situation to her sister's, and each was made miserable by what she felt she lacked and the sister had.

These tactics are also seen in the story of Miriam and Aaron's confrontation with Moses in Numbers 12. The two siblings of Moses could not stand the fact that their brother was "the" leader of Israel and coveted that same recognition.

We see these tactics used in 1 Samuel 18, where a young David was praised by the people for his military victories, and this recognition of David's triumphs made Saul so bitter that he later attempted to kill David.

These tactics are illustrated in Corinthians, where the believers were eager to claim that the leader each of them followed was the greatest. Paul challenged them in their divisiveness, writing, "Since there is jealousy and quarreling among you, are you not worldly? Are you not acting like mere men?" (1 Corinthians 3:3).

Yet again we see these tactics illustrated in Philippians, where an imprisoned Paul recognized that some "[preached] Christ out of envy and rivalry" (Philippians 1:15). They were driven by false motives to do something that seemed right and good, but underlying their actions was a desire to surpass their rivals.

It may be rooted in fallen human nature to be eaten up by jealousy. It may be rooted in fallen human nature to become bitter over another's success, or to be filled with self-pity when we compare what we have with what others have. It may be rooted in human nature to compete with someone viewed as a rival. But Satan takes full advantage of our vulnerabilities. He attempts constantly to overcome with evil the good in God's gift of our uniqueness.

No wonder one of the Ten Commandments is this: "You shall not covet" (Exodus 20:17). And this Commandment is developed more fully than most of the others. There is no place for coveting (envying) a neighbor's house or spouse or employees or ox, which represented wealth in ancient Israel, or "anything that belongs to your neighbor."

The message is this: Be satisfied not only with what you have, but also with who you are. You are not your neighbor.

You do not live his or her life. You live your own life. And because God has fashioned the unique "you" that you are, you are to be comfortable with yourself, and content.

A Visit to Joy

Joy was born while I was a student at Dallas Theological Seminary. In the hospital my wife suffered a massive placental separation, and even though the doctors acted quickly, there was a period of time when Joy had no access to oxygen.

At first we noticed nothing unusual about her. She seemed to be a happy baby, although she did not respond to us as her older brother had. But within six months we realized that something was radically wrong. Joy was diagnosed with severe brain damage. She would develop normally physically. But with her diminished mental capacity she would never be able to live a normal life. She would need someone to care for her all her days.

Today, at age 51, Joy lives in a family setting with a retired social worker and Becky, who is more severely disabled than Joy. Yet Joy is a happy person. She cares for herself, and especially cares for Becky, whose frequent seizures Joy senses before they strike. Joy loves to go to church, sings hymns and prays. She loves to eat out at the local pancake house, and take the family dogs for short walks. Joy is perfectly happy with the little she has: her bed, her room, her TV and, recently, a cell phone her caregiver keeps so Joy will not lose it.

Would Joy have had a different life if she had not been disabled? Of course. But today we can see clearly that Joy is the unique individual God intended her to be, a loving, caring person who enjoys the life she lives and who loves those who love her. Today I recognize God's goodness in leading us to both of the names we gave her at birth: *Joy* and *Grace*.

Overcoming Evil with Good

The New Testament has three primary images for the New Testament faith community. Christ's Church is a family (see Ephesians 3:14–19). Christ's Church is a body, a living organism (see 1 Corinthians 12). And Christ's Church is a royal priesthood (see 1 Peter 2:4–10). It is in the image of the Christian community as the Body of Christ that we see most clearly the importance of individual uniqueness.

As the Old Testament helps us understand God's role in shaping each person to be unique, so the New Testament affirms powerfully the significance of uniqueness. Paul begins his introduction to this theme by stating that "the body is a unit, though it is made up of many parts" (1 Corinthians 12:12). He goes on to point out that in a body each part—hand, eye, ear, etc.—has its own function. Paul then makes this startling statement: "But in fact God has arranged the parts in the body, every one of them, just as he wanted them to be" (verse 18).

Earlier in that chapter Paul points out that "to each one the manifestation of the Spirit is given for the common good" (verse 7). Not only has God been involved personally in shaping the persons we become, He has also given us the spiritual gifts that fit us for our roles in the Body "just as He wanted."

Later Paul deals with the potential jealousy and envy that might result from these differences. He writes that

> those parts of the body that seem to be weaker are indispensable, and the parts that we think are less honorable we treat with special honor. . . . God has combined the members of

the body and has given greater honor to the parts that lacked it, so that there should be no division in the body, but that its parts should have equal concern for each other.

1 Corinthians 12:22–25

The truth is that not only is each of us unique, each in our uniqueness is an indispensable part of the Body of Christ. The grandmother who works in the church nursery is no less important than the world-renowned evangelists. The shy individual who prays faithfully for others is to be honored as much as the soprano gifted with a voice that fills others' hearts with praise for the Lord.

The apostle Paul wanted the Corinthians to understand this, because their community had been marked by "jealousy and quarreling" (1 Corinthians 3:3). Factions argued over which leader was more important, even though God shaped and gifted individuals in such a way that "there should be no division in the body." Satan was using the fact that each of them was unique to destroy the unity of the Body. Satan was using uniqueness to stimulate jealousy, envy, bitterness, pride and self-pity.

No Division

The Body of Christ is an organism, whose members are directed to maintain unity. Satan's strategy is to promote divisiveness among us in an effort to overcome the good of our uniqueness with evil. The Bible shows us how to counter this attempt.

Repudiate superiority. The cause of divisions in the Corinthian Christian community was an intense desire to feel superior. Paul pointed out to them that, in their community, "not many of you were wise by human standards; not many were influential; not many were of noble birth" (1 Corinthians

1:26). Since there was nothing particularly special about themselves, the Corinthians tried to build their sense of superiority by emphasizing their allegiance to one well-known Christian leader or another. Instead of finding their common identity in relationship with Jesus, they tried to distinguish themselves from their brothers and sisters, and claimed superiority based on the leaders they associated themselves with.

The practice hardly stopped with the Corinthians. Even today some of us feel a sense of superiority based on the denomination we are associated with and the doctrines it emphasizes. While we should be committed to the fellowship and teaching within our denominations, this does not make us superior in any way to Christian brothers or sisters who express some aspects of faith and practice differently. We are united by our shared personal relationship with Jesus, and with Paul we can say: "Let him who boasts boast in the Lord" (1 Corinthians 1:31).

But what about those who actually have some basis upon which to feel superior? Paul said there were "not many" wise or influential or of noble birth. That meant there were some, and Christians are as susceptible as any other group to measuring the importance of people solely on their status in secular society.

The apostle James provides us with a good illustration. He describes a situation where a poor man in shabby clothes and a rich man in fine clothes both visit a church. The rich man is given special attention and the poor man allotted a seat on the floor. James writes bluntly, "If you show favoritism, you sin" (James 2:9).

Back in Corinthians, Paul addressed the specific situation by comparing his ministry to that of another leader, Apollos, and saying,

I have applied these things to myself and Apollos for your benefit, so that you may learn from us the meaning of the saying, "Do not go beyond what is written." Then you will not take pride in one man over against another. For who makes you different from anyone else? What do you have that you did not receive? And if you did receive it, why do you boast as though you did not?

1 Corinthians 4:6–7

God is the source of our uniqueness and of the spiritual gifts we have been given. We may praise God for this. But we can never claim to be superior to any Christian brother or sister.

Honor one another. Paul picked up the theme of unity in uniqueness again when writing to the Philippians. Paul urged the Philippians to "make my joy complete by being like-minded, having the same love, being one in spirit and purpose." Paul went on to explain what this involves: "Do nothing out of selfish ambition or vain conceit [that is, repudiate the notion of superiority], but in humility consider others better than yourselves" (Philippians 2:3).

This calls for a total reversal in the attitude we generally take toward ourselves and others. Instead of striving to establish our own importance to the destruction of unity in the Body, we should live in humility and view others in their uniqueness as "better than ourselves."

The Greek word translated here "better than" is *hyper-echo*, and occurs only five times in the New Testament. Each time it is translated by different words or phrases that seem to have little in common. It is best understood here to emphasize significance rather than superiority. When we emphasize the fact that others truly count, we will act as the next verse directs: "Each of you should look not only to your own interests, but also to the interests of others" (Philippians 2:4). When each of us sees the other in his or her uniqueness as truly counting in the Body of Christ, we become humble and experience unity "in spirit and purpose."

While Paul's focus in this passage is on attitude, attitude translates into truly significant action. Over the centuries of the Christian era, denominations and churches became increasingly hierarchical. Significant ministries became the province of pastors and bishops, and the laity were employed primarily to maintain the functioning of churches as institutions. In the same way significant ministries in the church were denied to women. But when we look again at an early Church gathering as described in the New Testament, we see that there "everyone has a hymn, or a word of instruction, a revelation, a tongue or an interpretation" (1 Corinthians 14:26). A similar picture is seen in Colossians 3:16, where Paul directed the people to "let the word of Christ dwell in you richly as you teach and admonish one another with all wisdom." And 1 Corinthians 11:5, in a passage that calls for propriety in worship services, Paul asked women to wear head coverings when they prayed or prophesied in church meetings.

It is our responsibility to honor the uniqueness not only of each person, but also of each person's gifts and placement in the Body of Christ.

Commit to servanthood. In the Philippians 2 passage, Paul's exhortation is followed by a powerful and poetic description of how Christ humbled Himself, abandoning His position in heaven, being born as a human being and undergoing death on a cross. And Paul says to the Body: "Your attitude should be the same as that of Christ Jesus" (Philippians 2:5).

Christ challenged His disciples concerning their attitudes. He called them together and said,

"You know that the rulers of the Gentiles lord it over them, and their high officials exercise authority over them. Not so with you. Instead, whoever wants to become great among you must be your servant, and whoever wants to be first must be your slave—just as the Son of Man did not come to be served, but to serve, and to give his life as a ransom for many."

Matthew 20:25–29

When we repudiate the idea that we are in some way superior to others, when we honor each other's uniqueness, and when we commit to using our uniqueness in service to others, we can and will overcome Satan's efforts to use our uniqueness for evil. We will overcome evil with good.

Being Comfortable with Uniqueness

1. Recognize the fact that God shaped you to be the unique person you are becoming.
2. Recognize the fact that God has gifted you for your unique role in the Body of Christ.
3. Avoid envy of who others are or what they have.
4. Be aware of and repudiate any desire to feel superior to others.
5. Always view and treat others as though they are special and significant. They truly are.
6. Focus on the interests and needs of others rather than on your own.
7. Make it your goal to serve others in any way you can.

12

The Gift of Provision

The day I met Clyde we went for a ride in his top-of-the-line Cadillac. I could not help thinking how much money it must have cost, and how that money could have been better used.

It was a foolish thought by a man who was old enough to know better. But I had been brought up in the home of a rural mail carrier during WWII, and while I never thought of us as poor, we certainly did not have much.

Later I saw just how foolish I was to have had such a thought about Clyde. He was a successful builder who had developed properties all over Florida. He now lived in Colorado, in the wealthy community of Evergreen in the mountains outside of Denver. His Cadillac, like the mansion he built, allowed him to fit into the community, and to relate to people who were as well off as he. People who would never have seen me as an equal, simply because I was not wealthy. The fact that Clyde and his wife, Joan, fit in made it possible for them to start a house church that reached many of his wealthy neighbors, and eventually grew so large it was necessary to meet in three spacious homes rather than one. And it enabled Joan to lead Bible studies for women of the community.

I learned, too, that Clyde had started what was called Dynamic Church Ministries, and later I joined him in conducting weeklong schools of ministry for pastors in half a dozen locations around the country. This was a ministry that Clyde financed with his own money.

How wrong I had been that first day to judge Clyde by his Cadillac! And what an ignorance of Scripture it showed.

It Was Good

The first verses of Scripture that describe how God shaped our universe repeat the words *and God saw that it was good*. The Hebrew word is *tob*, and here, as often in the Old Testament, it has no moral connotations. Rather *good* means "beautiful" or "pleasing," and includes the idea of prosperity and plenty.

It was as part of this material universe that God created human beings. We stand with one foot in the spiritual universe, created with an innate awareness of God, and with the other foot in the physical universe, living out our lives on this earth. The good, beautiful and pleasing things of earth are gifts of God—actively provided by Him—and important to us. David expressed it this way:

> You care for the land and water it; you enrich it abundantly. The streams of God are filled with water to provide the people with grain, for so you have ordained it. You drench its furrows and level its ridges; you soften it with showers and bless its crops.
>
> Psalm 65:9–10

David viewed God as one who "satisfies [our] desires with good things" (Psalm 103:5). The apostle Paul explained to Timothy that "everything God created is good, and nothing is to be rejected if it is received with thanksgiving" (1 Timothy 4:4).

At the moment, my wife and I are considering "downsizing." At our age, with no children in the home, we have far more space than we need. But it is hard to decide what to abandon. Not that anything is worth a lot of money—but there is that vase my wife got from her grandmother, and that sofa and chair that stood in my dad's house. And what about my fishing poles, hanging on their racks in the garage? Even though I doubt that I will ever do much fishing again, they, like the vase and the sofa, are part of our history, and in a sense part of our identity.

This world is filled with good things, practical gifts that God has designed to meet our needs, and pleasure gifts that are to be enjoyed with thanksgiving. Everything God has created *is* good, and God expresses His goodness to us by all that our earth supplies. Even more, Jesus reminds us that the good God has provided is for all, for "he causes his sun to rise on the evil and the good, and sends rain on the righteous and the unrighteous" (Matthew 5:45).

Limited Goods

It is hard for us to imagine what it was like to live in Bible times. One reason is that within an agricultural economy, the peoples of both the Old and New Testaments lived in an age of limited goods. That is, the land produced a limited amount of wealth, and that wealth had to be distributed among the people who lived in the land. If we call the total amount available to be distributed 100 percent, and if it was distributed equally, each family might expect, say, .0001 percent of the total goods.

But the wealth was not distributed equally. Some in society received far more than their "fair" share. These were the rich, or wealthy, of the New Testament, and it was clear to all they gained their wealth by exploiting those who were poorer. That is why James challenged believers who showed favoritism to the wealthy, saying, "You have insulted the poor. Is it not the rich who are exploiting you?" (James 2:6).

Today we live in a period of unlimited goods. An individual can invent an iPad and become enormously wealthy without taking an unfair share of the pool of wealth in the economy. In fact, his invention might add greatly to that pool of wealth. But what remains the same is the desire of some to have more and more of the good things God has provided for all. And this clearly is the basis of Satan's strategies to overcome this good with evil.

A Test Case

One of sacred history's great men is Solomon, who told his personal story in the book of Ecclesiastes. He had determined to put life to a test and "find out what is good."

> I undertook great projects: I built houses for myself and planted vineyards. I made gardens and parks and planted all kinds of fruit trees in them. I made reservoirs to water groves of flourishing trees. I bought male and female slaves and had other slaves who were born in my house. I also owned more herds and flocks than anyone in Jerusalem before me. I amassed silver and gold for myself, and the treasure of kings

and provinces. I acquired men and women singers, and a harem as well—the delights of the heart of man. I became greater by far than anyone in Jerusalem before me.

Ecclesiastes 2:4–9

Yet at the end of his life as Solomon looked back over all he had done and experienced, he concluded that "everything was meaningless, a chasing after the wind; nothing was gained under the sun" (Ecclesiastes 2:11).

Solomon had searched most of his life to discover a simple truth that Jesus relayed to a man who asked Him to broker the division of the family inheritance with a brother: "Watch out! Be on your guard against all kind of greed; a man's life does not consist in the abundance of his possessions" (Luke 12:15).

Satan's Strategy Exposed

Satan's basic strategy is to convince people that a person's life *does* consist in the abundance of his possessions. The material things God has provided for us are good. But Satan all too often succeeds in twisting our desire for God's good gifts into something evil.

The first tactic is to focus a person's attention on his wealth and create a burning desire for more. Solomon commented on this, noting that "whoever loves money never has money enough; whoever loves wealth is never satisfied with his income." As a person who had lived just such a life, Solomon concluded, "This too is meaningless" (Ecclesiastes 5:10).

The prophet Habakkuk wrote about an even more painful consequence for the one driven by wealth: "He is arrogant and never at rest," the prophet said. "He is as greedy as the grave and like death is never satisfied" (Habakkuk 2:5). What a tragedy, to spend one's life in a frantic effort to accrue riches, never realizing that that passion makes it impossible to know peace and satisfaction!

Satan is glad to accommodate those whose passion is to acquire wealth, because he is robbing them of what is truly important.

The second tactic is to convince people that wealth is enough. Wealth can and often does blind the wealthy to spiritual realities. They have more than they will ever need for this life, and pay no attention to their relationship with God. After all, they are rich. Why would they need God?

Remember the personal battle with envy that plagued the psalmist Asaph: "[The wicked] are free from the burdens common to man," he lamented. "Always carefree, they increase in wealth" (Psalm 73:5, 12). But then Asaph realized that his personal situation forced him to keep depending on the Lord. The wealthy person's situation is just the opposite; he sees no need to depend on God. This, Asaph realized, is "slippery ground."

The third tactic is to use wealth to corrupt a person's character. The prophet Amos painted an extensive portrait of the way the rich of his day exploited the poor: "You trample on the poor and force him to give you grain. . . . You oppress the righteous and take bribes and you deprive the poor of justice in the courts" (Amos 5:11–12).

In some strange way, wealth can rob an individual of concern for others, and lead him to "trample on the poor." The apostle Paul's comments on an ungodly attitude toward wealth are given in 1 Timothy 6:9–10:

> People who want to get rich fall into temptation and a trap and into many foolish and harmful desires that plunge men

into ruin and destruction. For the love of money is a root of all kinds of evil. Some people, eager for money, have wandered from the faith and pierced themselves with many griefs.

The fourth tactic Satan uses is to stir up envy in the majority who are not wealthy, and to glamorize the "beautiful people." If Satan can get us to focus on what we do not have, rather than be thankful for what we do have, he has found yet another way to overcome one of God's good gifts with evil.

Overcoming Evil with Good

It is important to maintain our perspective when dealing with wealth. The desire for wealth, or any material thing that God calls "good," can be twisted into evil by Satan. God challenged Israel in Deuteronomy 8:18 with these words: "Remember the Lord your God, for it is he who gives you the ability to produce wealth."

Clyde was one of those people who had a God-given ability to produce wealth. As a child he set out to raise money by collecting empty soda bottles on which there was a deposit. Each afternoon he pulled a wagon through his neighborhood and to nearby construction sites, collecting bottles. He set himself a daily goal, and was almost frantic if it seemed he would miss it.

As a young adult Clyde moved to Florida to join his uncle's garage-building business. But this was not enough for Clyde. One day he and his wife called on a woman who owned orange orchards. Despite his youth and lack of funds or experience, he left the home with a commitment to purchase the land. Clyde's first development on that land led to the building of thousands of homes in Florida, and made Clyde a millionaire.

Clyde had been brought up in a Christian home and was a believer. He joined a church in Clearwater, Florida, but like many wealthy individuals he used his wealth to control what was happening in the congregation. In time God showed Clyde how arrogant and ungodly this was, and Clyde became committed to a servant style of leadership. Christ's community of faith could not be run like a corporation, nor dominated by a wealthy individual. The discovery caused a revolution in Clyde's attitude, and led him to invest much of his wealth in helping Christian leaders across the United States and Canada develop a more biblical approach to church leadership.

God had given Clyde the ability to produce wealth. And God had led a responsive and godly Clyde to invest that wealth in strengthening the Church. Then in Evergreen, Colorado, Clyde and a few friends launched a house church, guided by careful attention to biblical principles of leadership, which saw many of Clyde and Joan's wealthy friends become believers. If you want to learn what Clyde did, the book we wrote together, *A Theology of Church Leadership*, is available on Amazon.

And, of course, I learned, too. Wealth can never be the measure of a man. And there is no brother or sister we cannot be comfortable with, whether he is rich or poor.

Guidelines for the Ordinary

Most of us are basically ordinary people. We have jobs. We earn enough money to provide our families with food and shelter, as well as televisions, school supplies and an occasional evening out. Most of us do not see ourselves as wealthy, although we have far more than most of the people living today. We are just ordinary people. And the Bible has a lot to say on this subject to the ordinary people of any era.

First, though, we need to remember that material blessings are essentially good, not bad. Look again at Paul's words: "Everything God created is good, and nothing is to be rejected if it is received with thanksgiving" (1 Timothy 4:4). We are called to enjoy God's gift of good things—pleasant, pleasurable and beautiful things—and to praise Him for His generosity.

Given this truth, we do need to heed the advice and the warnings given in Scripture. Proverbs 30:8–9, for instance, makes an important point:

> "Give me neither poverty nor riches, but give me only my daily bread. Otherwise, I may have too much and disown you and say, 'Who is the Lord?' Or I may become poor and steal, and so dishonor the name of my God."

Paul certainly agreed with the main point: "Godliness with contentment is great gain. . . . If we have food and clothing, we will be content with that" (1 Timothy 6:6, 8).

There are many passages we can find that encourage the wealthy to be generous, and that speak out against the use of wealth to gain status, even in the church (see 1 Corinthians 11:17–22). In the same way Christians are exhorted not to live off others' labor, but to "settle down and earn the bread they eat" (2 Thessalonians 3:12).

Many portions of Scripture offer insight about wealth and possessions, as well as poverty, but there is one passage that seems to say it all.

Jesus' Teaching on the Mount

In His Sermon on the Mount, Jesus emphasized the fact that we should view God as a loving Father. When His disciples asked how to pray, He told them to say, "Give us today our daily bread" (Matthew 6:11)—not "Give us wealth." Jesus reminded them that it is foolish to "store up for yourselves treasures on earth." Such treasures cannot be protected, nor will they last. Instead of earthly treasures, Jesus said to focus on the heavenly treasures won by serving God. This is a definite and defining choice, for "no one can serve two masters. Either he will hate [decisively reject] the one and love [be fully committed to] the other, or he will be devoted to the one and despise the other. You cannot serve both God and Money" (verse 24).

It may seem to some a dangerous course. Are we not to focus on even the necessities of life in this world? Jesus said that God is our Father, and we are much more valuable to Him than the creatures who depend on Him for food, and the flowers that depend on Him for drapery. It is because we understand that God is not only *a* Father but *our* Father that we can be fully committed to Him. And it is because we know how valuable we are as His children that we can be comfortable focusing on serving Him. As Jesus expressed it, God knows that we need many of the things pagans spend their lives pursuing. When we put God's Kingdom and His righteousness first, all these things will be given to us as well.

Jesus summed up His teaching this way: "Therefore do not worry about tomorrow, for tomorrow will worry about itself" (Matthew 6:34). We need not live each day focused on wealth or material possessions—or even on necessities—but rather on committing ourselves daily to doing the will of God.

Putting Material Goods into Perspective

1. Express thanks to God daily for the material goods He has provided for you.
2. Avoid making decisions based solely on the amount of money you will save or gain.
3. Thank God for the abundance He has given others. This will help you curb any envy or jealousy.
4. If God has given you the ability to produce wealth, share it generously with others who are in need.
5. Do not look for meaning or fulfillment in the material possessions that you gather.
6. Determine not to use your relative wealth to gain an advantage over another person.
7. Always remember that God is your Father, and that He loves you.
8. Make a decisive choice between serving God or money. You cannot serve both.

13

The Gift of Truth

We arrived at Saguaro Lake in the late afternoon. The lake was one of my favorite fishing spots, just 45 minutes or so from our Phoenix home.

My two sons and a neighborhood friend of theirs and I were planning an overnight fishing trip. The lake, which I had fished often, glowed with the reflection of the setting sun as I motored our boat deeper and deeper into winding canyons. When it got too dark to see farther, we drew up to the shore.

My younger son, Tim, and the neighbor child, Kirk, got off the boat to explore. I could hear them running in the grasses that grew deep along the shore. Then I heard a cry of pain. Kirk, frightened, was running back to the boat. I quickly reached Tim, who was hobbling slowly toward us. There was a long gash running along his shin, bleeding profusely. Someone had once fenced off a section of land with barbed wire, and Tim had tripped and fallen on a barb that had torn deeply into his flesh. It was clear that he needed stitches, and soon.

We got into the boat and I headed back toward the launch site. But very quickly I became disoriented. I knew the lake well, but that was in daylight. On that black Arizona night I could hardly make out the bluffs and buttes that marked my waypoints along the canyon lake. Before long I was totally confused. Where were we? And how was I to get my bleeding son the emergency medical treatment he needed?

Welcome to Satan's World

One of the most significant theological terms in the New Testament is *kosmos*. It occurs some 180 times in Scripture, and in 173 cases is translated "world." Its classical meaning was "order" or "arrangement." As a theological term, *kosmos* represents human cultures as they are arranged by the perspectives, values, attitudes and behaviors of a lost humanity. The Bible makes it clear that this arrangement is supervised by Satan himself. Thus, the apostle John tells us that "the whole world is under the control of the wicked one" (1 John 5:19). The values, the beliefs, the attitudes that dominate in our societies are controlled by Satan.

Recalling my experience that night on Saguaro Lake made me think of that verse in 1 John. I was lost in the darkness, confused about which way to go. Today so many in our culture are just as confused, just as uncertain about the choices they are called on to make.

John has much more to say about the world system controlled by Satan. Take 1 John 2:15–17:

Do not love the world or anything in the world. If anyone loves the world, the love of the Father is not in him. For everything in the world—the cravings of sinful man, the lust of his eyes and the boasting of what he has and does—comes not from the Father but from the world. The world and its desires pass away, but the man who does the will of God lives forever.

The patterns that Satan devises for human cultures appeal to the cravings of our sinful humanity, to the desires stimulated by what we see and to pride based on what we have or do. Later John notes that the spirit of the antichrist infuses some, who "are from the world and therefore speak from the viewpoint of the world, and the world listens to them" (1 John 4:5). We all tend to make choices approved of by others, who "speak from the viewpoint of the world."

Desperate for Direction

This does not mean for a moment that every individual on earth is consciously or intentionally wicked. But Proverbs 14:12 reminds us that "there is a way that seems right to a man, but in the end it leads to death." That word *right* is *yasarl* in the Hebrew. It occurs 117 times in the Old Testament, and 92 of those times is translated "upright" or "right." It suggests that many people honestly want to do what is right for them and for others. The trouble is that the choices they end up making are too often wrong choices, and lead to disaster.

Let's consider this in a situation that is common in our world. According to a Livescience.com survey, 75 percent of women in America under the age of thirty have lived (cohabited) with someone at some time. In most of those cases there was an original expectation of marriage somewhere down the line. But the belief that "if we love each other, it's all right" permeates modern America and many other cultures.

The consequences of this and similar choices are felt by many children who now live in single parent homes. According to the Kids Count Data Center, in America this includes 67 percent of African American children, 42 percent of Hispanic children and 25 percent of non-Hispanic white children. Granted, these statistics include homes of widows and widowers who are single parents by default, or individuals who tried to hold their families together in the face of divorce. But in the vast majority of these instances, the couples choose not to marry, and one of the parents is usually left to raise the children alone.

It is impossible to tell how many men and women have come to the end of their lives only to realize that their choices deprived them of relationship within the core community of marriage and hampered close connections with their children.

The world around us is constantly urging us to pursue courses that are driven by "the cravings of sinful man, the lust of his eyes and the boasting of what he has and does." Like me that night on Saguaro Lake, people find no clear waypoints guiding to what is right. And so they choose courses that "seem right," unable to judge what the consequences will be.

That night on Saguaro Lake, while trying desperately to get our bearings and see which way to go, we found another fisherman. He told us our position on the lake, and pointed the way to the launch.

Soon I was winching the boat back onto its trailer, and getting Tim to the hospital emergency room. Once I knew the way, everything was all right.

Know the Way

This is something most believers do not quite understand about *truth*. In Scripture, truth is not just something to be believed. Truth is a revelation of reality.

The Hebrew word for *truth* is *'emet*. It comes from a root meaning "to be established, certain or faithful." It can be translated both "true" and "faithful," and, thus, what is true is totally reliable. When the psalmist asks God to send forth His truth to guide him (see Psalm 43:3), he views truth as a reliable guide to life. What is true cuts through the illusions cast by Satan over the world in the invisible war, and enables us to make choices that are in harmony with reality.

The Greek word translated "truth" has the same general meaning. When used in theologically sensitive passages, "the truth" encompasses all of reality as God knows it and has revealed it. In the *Encyclopedia of Bible Words*, I summarize it this way:

> God has cleared away humanity's illusory beliefs and notions and in the gospel has provided a clear perspective on reality. Through revelation we at last have reliable knowledge about God, about ourselves, about the nature of the universe, and most importantly about how to live in intimate relationship with the Lord.

p. 602

As this paragraph suggests, truth is not just something to be believed, as reliable doctrine. Truth is divine revelation that serves as a guide to how life is to be lived. Commenting on 1 John 1:6, which says that we have fellowship with God when we "live by truth," the encyclopedia continues:

John constantly calls us to adopt the divine perspective provided for us in Christ and in God's Word. As we refuse to live self-deceiving and deceitful lives, but rather commit ourselves to act by faith on those things that God says are real, we will personally experience truth and find our heritage of freedom.

p. 603

Satan's Strategy Exposed

Satan understands human nature. He knows what appeals to us, what drives us and those things in which we take pride. And Satan has used this knowledge to shape human cultures to appeal to that nature.

We would be mistaken if we thought Satan was interested in driving humans to become as sinful and evil as possible. Satan is satisfied to encourage an individual to live what the individual believes is a "good life"—just as long as the choices that "seem right" to that person are measured by cultural values and driven by the old sin nature.

Satan's basic strategy, then, is both to blind us to truth, and to provide pseudo truths to act on in its place.

The first tactic is to erode the concept of truth. We live in a culture today where the idea of absolutes is rejected. Rather than *truth*, there are "truths," which vary from individual to individual. Something may be "true for you" that is not "true for me." The fact that I believe marriage involves a lifelong commitment between a man and a woman can be treated as my "truth," while the belief that two same-sex partners may be married can be someone else's "truth." In this case, truth is viewed subjectively. There is no absolute standard of right and wrong to which either of us can appeal.

At the same time, the legitimate influence of authority—in the sense of beneficial guidance that comes through proven experience or tradition—is rapidly being eroded. Back in the 1960s in America, for instance, the "anti-establishment" drug culture opposed many conventional social and political mores. Today, however, we are witnessing in the generation known as the Millennials (those born in the years from 1978–1995) almost complete disinterest in all traditional authority figures—and rejection of the concept of authority itself. In this new wave of "freedom," each person is encouraged to make his or her own decisions, without the encumbrance of traditional beliefs, experience or even reason.

This leads to *the second tactic*: to develop dependence on one's peer group. If the wisdom available from traditional authorities, those with proven experience, is rejected, where can one look for advice? Looking again at those in the Millennial generation, we often see that when they need to make a decision, they trust only peers—those who are going through the same kinds of experiences they are—to give relevant advice.

Recently, for example, I heard of a young woman who wanted to buy a new car. She sent out a request for help to her two hundred Facebook "friends." Then she went out and bought the car (even in the color) chosen by her "friends."

True, Millennials are often described as being a socially responsible generation, and, no doubt, some of those "friends" gave good nuts-and-bolts technical details about various cars. But it shows the sole reliance on social peers that is growing in our society.

Look at the difference that has come in just a generation or two. My wife and I were looking for a car to lease and followed the more traditional approach that has generally guided decision-making up till the present day. We read reviews by experts that described in detail the cars and SUVs we were interested in, identifying their strengths and weaknesses. Then we went to a dealer and test-drove the few that we felt met our needs and budget. We welcomed personal "testimonies" from those who owned those particular vehicles, and made our decision based on all those factors.

This approach of looking to "authorities" or the voice of experience is slowly disappearing. The "peer only" approach is helping to shape culture into accepting a relativistic perception of truth in which traditional wisdom is rejected.

The third tactic is to encourage the idea that the only way a person can tell if a course of action will help or harm is to take that action and see the results. This is closely related to the idea that what is "true for you" need not be "true for me." You might choose, as did a woman known by a young friend of mine, to marry "because he's the only one I know who can satisfy me," and inherit a disaster. But someone else might choose to marry for the same reason, and live happily ever after. The only way to know, Satan has convinced many, is to go ahead and do what you want, and see how it works out.

This particular notion is illustrated by the generations that have taken up and given force to the age-old mantra that "Everybody's doing it!" Take the invitation to try "harmless" drugs, like marijuana. The marijuana harvested today is far more potent than that smoked in the '60s, and has been proven to affect the brain adversely. Evidence of its damage is clear. But the idea has gotten a grip today that the only way really to know is to try it, and see how it affects us. "Do what you want," Satan beckons. "It's the only way to know for sure."

These three tactics of Satan, which are directed primarily at non-Christians, mingle to make his attack on truth more effective. There is no *truth*, only truths. None of the traditional authorities can be trusted, and indeed must be rejected. The only people I can rely on for guidance are members of my peer group, who are struggling with the same issues I am. Ultimately, the only way I can find out if something will help or harm me is to try it and find out for myself. The result, of course, is that millions make decisions that "seem right" to them, unaware that this approach to making moral choices can "lead to death" in the end.

But Satan is far too wise to limit his attempts to nonbelievers. Satan has a strategy that is ready-made for Christians of any age. *The fourth tactic* is to encourage the idea that *truth* is basically about what we believe.

As Christians we believe in the virgin birth, the crucifixion and the resurrection of Jesus. We believe that salvation is by faith alone, and that when Jesus returns we will be caught up and forever be with Him. These doctrines—*truth*—are revealed in Scripture, and we believe them. It is comfortable, going to church and knowing that we believe the right things. There are times, granted, that we Christians debate whether various other ideas held as doctrines by other Christians are truth or simply opinion. But all Christians affirm Jesus as God the Son, and hold that the key to salvation is to establish a personal relationship with Jesus through faith.

We see these central doctrines defined clearly in Scripture as *truth*. And they are. But Scripture reveals that there is far more to this concept. If we limit our idea of truth to doctrines, Satan has succeeded in actually distorting our understanding of what truth is and what it means for us. Let me show you what I mean.

Overcoming Evil with Good

The debate between Jesus and a group of Pharisees was growing heated. They challenged Jesus' claim of divinity, and He challenged their claim that, as descendants of Abraham, they had a relationship with God. If God truly was the Father of these religious men, Jesus told them, "you would love me, for I came from God" (John 8:42). The leaders accused Christ of being demon-possessed; Jesus said their response to Him revealed that "you belong to your father, the devil," who was a murderer and liar from the beginning, "and you want to carry out your father's desire" (John 8:44). No one won the debate that day, but very shortly the Pharisees proved Jesus right: They engineered Christ's murder on the cross.

During the confrontation with the Pharisees, Jesus spoke also to those who believed in Him. He said, "If you hold to my teaching, you are really my disciples. Then you will know the truth, and the truth will set you free" (John 8:31–32). The meaning of *hold to* is "put into practice." And the promise is that a disciple who lives out Jesus' teachings will "know the truth."

There are two primary Greek words for *know*. One refers to innate or abstract knowledge. The other identifies knowledge rooted in personal experience. There is vast difference between them. A teen who completes the classwork portion of a driver-education course and claims "I know how to drive" might be right. But the claim to "know how to drive" is very different when made by his parents, who have actually been driving for twenty or thirty years. The teen's "knowledge" is intellectual. The parents' knowledge is experiential.

The word that Jesus used on that occasion focuses our attention on knowledge gained by personal experience. Jesus was saying this: "If you put My teachings into practice, then you will experience the truth. And that experience will set you free."

In Scripture *truth* is a reliable and accurate description of reality. We are not called simply to believe the truth—the doctrines—revealed in the Bible. We are called to put Jesus' teachings into practice daily. We are called to make God's revealed truth the standard by which we measure those things that "seem right," and the standard that guides our own choices and decisions. We are called to rely on God's revelation of what is good and what is right.

When we commit to being a disciple of Jesus, taking His words as the authoritative standard by which to measure our actions and make our choices, we then and only then will truly know (experience) the world as God intends us to live in it.

Jesus concluded with a second promise. If we put His words into practice, we will not only experience reality as God knows it, but we will find that a life lived in harmony with the way things really are will set us free.

The Truth about Truth

It might seem strange. But people of any generation who seek freedom by rejecting absolutes and relying on others as lost as themselves to define right and wrong are people in chains. They are people bound by Satan, and led by him into illusion after illusion. They seek liberation, but they are being enticed further away from it.

As with most schemes of Satan, this trend against truth is growing in our society. And believers, young or old, are just as susceptible as unbelievers, young or old. When you and I assume that we know the truth because we believe all the right things, we have fallen victim to one of Satan's tactics to overcome the good God intended. We are ourselves rejecting an absolute—the truth of Scripture—and missing the freedom offered there.

Only as we are committed to following Jesus can we experience all that God has in store for us. Only as we are committed to following Jesus can we make choices that will bring benefit rather than harm. When we realize that *truth* reveals reality as only God knows, then we will be able to step out boldly to follow Jesus and to act on His Word—and that truth will make us truly free.

Learning to Live the Truth

1. Examine closely the basis for the choices you have been making.
2. Be especially wary of unexamined choices that reflect what "everyone is doing" or what "everyone says."
3. Make a commitment not simply to believe in Jesus, but to be His disciple and to put His teachings into practice daily.
4. Read what Jesus said in Matthew 6. Make a list of the attitudes and values taught in this chapter of Scripture. How are you doing as a disciple? What do you need to bring into closer conformity with Jesus' words?
5. Make a list of biblical doctrines you believe. Then try to identify one way each doctrine has had an impact on your daily life.

—14—

The Gift of Peace

We learned from Genesis 1 that God likes order. He fashioned our world so that day follows night, and season follows season. We are comfortable with this. We want our lives to be predictable. We want to wake up in the morning to sunlight, have our coffee, read a brief devotional and watch *Good Morning America* for a few minutes before we go off to work. Like the God who created us in His image, we feel at peace when our personal world is orderly, stable and marked by consistency.

Satan, however, is committed to chaos. He delights in disorder, uncertainty and the stress of the frighteningly unpredictable. Satan is eager to turn our world upside down, as we see in the classic example of how he overturned the world of a man named Job. That good man lived a stable, predictable and blessed life. But when God removed the hedge He had placed around His servant, Satan pounced. In a single day Job lost his wealth, his children and his health. Finally his wife told him just to curse God and die. Job's comfortable, stable world was gone, and he was filled with doubt and terror. Why had God done this to him? But it was not God. It was Satan, bringing chaos through the frighteningly unpredictable.

We know the end of the story. All Satan had taken from Job was restored, and with it came a new sense of personal relationship with God. But that is the *end* of the story. Job suffered agony before he reached that place of peace.

God may permit Satan to bring chaos into our lives, too. But we do not have to live with the pain Job experienced. Jesus offers us the gift of peace.

"My Peace I Give You"

It was the night Jesus was betrayed. He was about to be taken before the Sanhedrin for a trial that was illegal according to Jewish law. Before that happened, Jesus prayed in the Garden of Gethsemane, a prayer felt so intensely that Christ would describe Himself as "overwhelmed with sorrow" (Matthew 26:38). Luke pictured the scene this way: "Being in anguish, he prayed more earnestly, and his sweat was like drops of blood falling to the ground" (Luke 22:44).

Although Jesus had predicted His death and knew what would happen, and even though it led to resurrection and a return to glory, the path was difficult. Yet this was the very night that Jesus told His disciples about a special gift He was giving them: the gift of peace. "Peace I leave with you," He said, "my peace I give you. I do not give to you as the world gives. Do not let your hearts be troubled and do not be afraid" (John 14:27).

What Jesus was describing is peace in the midst of chaos. It is peace that we experience even if at the same time we feel overwhelmed with anguish and uncertainty.

This peace is contrasted with the peace that the world gives. In John's writings *the world* is a theological term for sinful human culture, with all its illusory beliefs and values. The peace the world gives depends on life proceeding smoothly. The physical universe God created provides the context in which it really is possible to live comfortable, predictable lives. As long as we feel we have control of our circumstances, we have the only kind of peace the world can provide. But when Satan comes with chaos, and we realize we have lost control, the kind of peace the world gives disappears. And our only recourse is to seek Jesus' peace.

Satan's Strategy Exposed

Satan wants to bring chaos into our experience. That was what he did with Job, manipulating circumstances so that Job's life was turned upside down. Sometimes Satan causes chaos on a grand scale, such as the hundreds of thousands in Africa and the Middle East being displaced by war and threatened with genocide. But Satan's demons may also cause chaos in our individual lives.

Carol, a friend of ours, had sensed her husband's increasing alienation. When she discovered he was having an affair, he moved out of their home and manipulated their two teenagers to move in with him. Now in the process of divorce, Carol is left penniless, without a job or money to pay even for utilities. And her husband's lawyer is set on gaining sole custody of the children for him. Carol's life has crumbled into chaos, and none of the world's prescriptions for peace offers any solace.

John is another friend. Working for a medical supply company, he was a top salesperson, earning in six figures. He had a large house and expensive cars, and he felt fully in control of his life. Then, unexpectedly, he was let go. Now, nearly two years later, he still has not been able to find work. He has been forced to raid his kids' college fund. He simply does not know what he can do to get back to what he had thought of as "normal" life.

Not every experience of cancer, loss, divorce or other tragedy is caused by demons, of course. But Satan seizes every opportunity he can in the invisible war to encourage chaos in our lives. Then his demons whisper into our ears and try to drive us to a response that will weaken our relationship with God.

The first tactic is to cause doubt. When tragedy or suffering comes, it is natural for us to ask, "Why me?" That was Job's response. He had tried to live a good life, and had always thought of God as fair. God Himself called Job "blameless and upright" (Job 1:8). In Job's mind, this meant that God was responsible to look out for him. And God had. But then disaster struck, one blow after another, and Job was driven to question God. Job had always thought of God as fair. But God had not treated him fairly.

The bulk of the book of Job is composed of Job's dialogues with three friends, as together they struggled with the question, "Why?" The friends decided that Job must have committed some terrible sin for God to bring such suffering into his life. Even while maintaining his innocence, Job's doubts about God grew deeper and deeper.

This response to chaos is one that Satan enjoys. We ask what we have done to deserve our suffering, and when we cannot pinpoint a sin or failure we blame God for being unfair. Satan's demons whisper in our ears that God must have abandoned us, that He simply does not care. The result is to doubt God and our relationship with Him. And our peace is stripped away.

The second tactic is to undermine trust. Abraham and Sarah had been promised a child. But as the years passed and they grew older and older, Sarah did not conceive. Finally Sarah could not stand to wait any longer. She urged Abraham to father a child with her servant, Hagar, a child that would be called Sarah's.

Reluctantly, Abraham did as his wife asked, and Hagar became pregnant. But it did not turn out the way Sarah had planned. Hagar treated her childless mistress with contempt, and some years later when Sarah did have a child, Hagar's son teased her child mercilessly. Even today, the Arab peoples, who came from Hagar's son, remain tireless enemies of Sarah's descendants, the Jews.

Filled with doubt and uncertainty, waiting so long for God to act, Abraham and Sarah had panicked. Rather than wait on God, the two had taken matters into their own hands. This, too, is a response Satan intends to stimulate by creating chaos. As our uncertainty and panic grow we are ripe for Satan's demons to whisper that we simply have to do something, anything. Anxiety is a companion of chaos, and as we become more and more anxious we are all too likely to abandon trust and take matters in our own hands—with disastrous effect. And our peace is stripped away.

The third tactic is to exaggerate guilt. As King David fled from his rebellious son, Absalom, he remembered what people had been saying. He wrote his thoughts of that time in Psalm 3:2: "Many are saying of me, 'God will not deliver him.'"

David understood their reasoning. His sin with Bathsheba was well known, as was his failure to deal with his son Amnon when he raped his half sister, or with Absalom when in revenge he organized the murder of Amnon. David was deeply aware of his own sin and failures, even though he had confessed to God and publicly as well. How ashamed he felt, after all God had done for him! He could hardly expect God to deliver him from his desperate situation.

This, too, is one of the things demons whisper when we find ourselves in chaos. "You've hurt others, and you have failed God terribly. You don't deserve God's help now. You are only getting what you deserve." As these thoughts take root, we are frozen, unable to act. And our peace is stripped away.

Rest for Your "Today"

David disappointed Satan. His kingdom was in chaos and he was fleeing for his life, but David lay down and slept, "because the LORD sustains me" (Psalm 3:5). He refused to fear the "tens of thousands drawn up against me on every side" (verse 6). David remembered all God had done for him in the past, and he was able to rest.

Rest is one of those very special words in Scripture. We can see how closely it is linked to the concept of peace. As we explore the concept of rest in the book of Hebrews, we come to understand the kind of peace Jesus experienced, and the kind of peace He gives. It is a peace that sustains us even as we are caught in the midst of chaos.

The writer of Hebrews introduces the concept of rest in chapters 3 and 4. He draws our attention back in time to when the Israelites were freed from slavery in Egypt on the way to Canaan, the land God had promised Abraham's descendants. For a people who had lived poverty-stricken lives in bondage, Canaan truly was the Promised Land. There, as God explained through Moses, they would live in "flourishing cities you did not build, houses filled with all kinds of good things you did not provide, wells you did not dig, and vineyards and olive groves you did not plant" (Deuteronomy 6:10–11). For an oppressed people, the prospect was stunning. Here was rest and peace at last.

But when the Israelites reached the borders of Canaan, they sent men ahead of them to reconnoiter it. Though the land was all that God had promised and more, the people who lived there were frighteningly tall and strong. And so the Israelites balked, and refused to enter the place of rest. God had promised to be with them, but they simply would not trust Him. God's response?

"I declared on oath in my anger, 'They shall never enter my rest'" (Hebrews 3:11). The result of the Israelites' refusal to enter the Promised Land was 38 years of wandering in the wilderness, until an entire generation died. Then their children did conquer Canaan.

But the writer of Hebrews sees more in the story than a history lesson. The story contains a promise: God intends to provide rest and peace for His people. Even in the midst of struggle, conflict and chaos, God invites us to be at rest.

The writer of Hebrews moves on to quote Psalm 95:7, where the psalmist says, "Today, if you hear his voice, do not harden your hearts as you did in the rebellion." To the writer of Hebrews that word *today* is significant. The fact that it recurs in David's psalm, "a long time later," is evidence that "there remains, then, a Sabbath-rest for the people of God" (Hebrews 4:9).

God has prepared a rest for us, as He prepared Canaan for the Israelites: a place where we can experience rest and peace. A generation of Israelites failed to find rest because, when they heard God's voice telling them to enter Canaan, they refused. The writer of Hebrews ascribes their response to "a sinful, unbelieving heart." They simply did not trust God.

It is no wonder that one of Satan's goals in causing chaos in our lives is to raise doubt and uncertainty about God and our relationship with Him. Anything that will keep us from responding to God's voice with trust for our own "today" is a victory for the evil one. By causing chaos, Satan seeks to overcome with evil the good of the peace available in Jesus. But however great the evils we experience, God holds out loving arms, inviting us to find peace and rest in Him. And the rest we are to find is the very rest that God Himself experiences.

Entering God's Rest

Again the writer of Hebrews looks back into sacred history. This time he looks to the Creation account. He recalls the words, "on the seventh day [God] rested from all his work" (Genesis 2:2). To the writer of Hebrews this implies that "his work has been finished since the creation of the world" (Hebrews 4:3), for if we read the Genesis account we realize that no evening is mentioned closing the seventh day, as evening closed the other six. For God, this is still the seventh day, and His work is finished.

This does not imply that God has been inactive. Far from it! God's miracles of judgment freed the Israelite slaves. He performed other wonders, opening a path through the sea for

Israel. He led his people in the wilderness by a cloudy-fiery pillar, and provided manna daily. And God remains actively involved in our lives today. What does it mean, then, that God "rested from all His work"?

The answer is simple. In creating our universe God looked ahead, and saw every possible situation that might arise. He foresaw every possible evil that Satan or his demons might perform, every possible choice that you or I might make, and every possible consequence. Without causing us to make this choice or that, God has prepared the way we are to take to find our way out of chaos. And God will speak to us in our "today," and show us what that way is.

It is no wonder, then, that we are told to rest from our own work, and to "make every effort to enter [God's] rest" (Hebrews 4:11). When we are caught up in chaos it is not our responsibility to discover our own way out. It is our responsibility simply to keep our eyes on the Lord, draw closer to Him and listen for His voice. When He speaks to us in our "today," we are to trust Him, and to obey.

This section of Hebrews closes with a powerful image, one that has often been misunderstood.

> For the word of God is living and active. Sharper than any double-edged sword, it penetrates even to dividing soul and spirit, joints and marrow; it judges the thoughts and attitudes of the heart. Nothing in all creation is hidden from God's sight. Everything is uncovered and laid bare before the eyes of him to whom we must give account.
>
> Hebrews 4:12–13

Frequently taken as a warning or even a threat, these words in this context are a stunning reminder of the depths of

God's love. They tell us that He knows each of us fully and completely. The implication is that when He speaks to us, the path He asks us to take will be one that has been shaped to fit each of us as individuals. The way through chaos will surely differ for each of us, for God takes into account every aspect of who we are as individuals, and took it into account long before we were born, from Creation itself.

Overcoming Evil with Good

Satan delights in chaos. He loves to turn our world upside down, to replace the comfortable and the familiar with the unpredictable and stressful. He thrills as we experience anxiety and fear. Through the chaos he creates or encourages, he hopes to see us question our belief in God, abandon trust and wallow hopelessly in guilt and shame.

The good that overcomes the evil Satan seeks to do through causing chaos is to look to Jesus for His peace. Peace sustained Jesus through the agonizing hours that led to the crucifixion. His peace will sustain us.

The peace Jesus knew was rooted in His knowledge that, even before the Creation, God was aware of what would happen. The peace we can know is rooted in the same reality. God created, and on the seventh day, He rested. Every possibility was foreseen, every emergency planned for. There is nothing that can overtake us that God has not known about, or that He is not prepared to guide us through.

And so we overcome the evil of chaos simply by keeping our eyes on the Lord, and listening for His voice, showing us our way.

Choosing Peace in the Midst of Chaos

1. Do not expect to live a stress-free, comfortable life. Times of chaos will come.
2. Do not take feelings of depression, hopelessness or anxiety as evidence that God has deserted you.
3. Consciously let Scripture shape your view of God. Read it to know Him better.
4. Do not settle for the peace the world gives. It never lasts.
5. Remember that God knows what is happening in your life, and knows the way through any painful situation you might be experiencing.
6. Guard against reacting to chaos with doubts about God, panic, hasty action, etc.
7. Be committed to obey when you hear God's voice in your "today." Trust Him, even though you might not understand why He is leading you as He is.

15

The Gift of Eternal Life, Now!

When I was in the navy, every morning I would go to my office early. I would type out a Bible verse and post it in the nook where the coffee was brewed. I called it "The verse of the day," and often hung around to see if it led to a conversation with my friends. There were two things particularly that bothered my navy buddies. One was the idea that anyone could know, absolutely know, he was going to heaven. The other was the idea that all our sins—past, present and future—are forgiven by Jesus.

"It just doesn't make sense," one of them told me. "If you know you'll be forgiven, you can go out and do anything you want to!"

My friend subscribed to the "If you weren't afraid of being punished, you'd sin gleefully" school of thought. The idea that you not only can be forgiven but *are* forgiven was too strange for him to comprehend.

It is not just non-Christians who are confused. The leader of our Monday night Bible study group, Allin, told me of eating a meal with a friend from a different church. They somehow got on to the topic of confessing sins, and the man told Allin that every night before he went to bed he confessed the day's sins to God. That way he would be sure to go to heaven if he died in his sleep.

Allin asked, "What if you committed a sin and were hit by a car before you could confess it? Would you go to heaven?"

The man thought for just a moment, and then said, "No, I'd go to hell."

To him and to members of his church, a confessed sin was forgiven, but any unconfessed sin damned a believer eternally.

Really?

It is fascinating to see the hesitation of many Christians when someone suggests that they have eternal life now. Somehow they cannot seem to take in the truth expressed in 1 John 5:1: "Everyone who believes that Jesus is the Christ is born of God." John addresses this further in verse 13: "I write these things to you who believe in the name of the Son of God so that you may know that you have eternal life."

John does not write, "So that you may know that *you will have* eternal life." He specifically wants his readers to realize that they *really have* eternal life, *now.*

Perhaps John's most powerful statement of this truth is found in 1 John 3:1–2:

How great is the love the Father has lavished on us, that we should be called children of God! And that is what we are! . . . Dear friends, now we are children of God, and what we will be has not yet been made known. But we know that when he appears, we shall be like him, for we shall see him as he is.

In all these verses we can hear echoes of Jesus teaching His disciples and the crowds: "I tell you the truth, whoever hears my word and believes him who sent me has eternal life and will not be condemned: he has crossed over from death to life" (John 5:24).

How could the message be clearer? Believers *have* eternal life. It is not that believers will have eternal life *then*. They have crossed over from death to life, and have eternal life *now*.

Satan's Strategy Exposed

Satan seems particularly bent on hiding this truth from Christians. His goal is to blind us to basic truths that free us to live a victorious Christian life. His strategy is to undermine our confidence in Christ with doubt and hesitation.

The first tactic is to suggest that our salvation is not permanent. For Allin's friend, he may have crossed over from death to life, but only his careful attention to confession of sins allowed him to retain salvation. He viewed salvation as something other than reliance on Christ alone. What he did or failed to do was an essential element in gaining, or retaining, salvation.

The belief that we can lose our salvation crops up over and over again in Christianity. Sometimes we are told that we must do something in addition to trusting in Jesus, such as undergo baptism or confess our sins. Sometimes we are warned that if we make a habit of some sin we will become "unsaved." Another view is a reaction to a specific promise Jesus made: "I give them eternal life, and they shall never perish; no one can snatch them out of my hand" (John 10:28). Well, they say, maybe no one can deprive a believer of his eternal life. But if a person recants after being saved, he can climb out of Jesus' hand himself!

Once again this ignores the truth Jesus was emphasizing. "I give them eternal life, and they *shall never perish*." That "they shall never perish" should settle the question once for all. But, as Satan did in Eden, he sows confusion by casting doubt on or denying God's Word.

Why is it so important to Satan to keep us from realizing that we have eternal life now? The answer is simple. As long as we remain unsure and anxious, our motives for whatever we do will be mixed at best. Jesus said: "If anyone loves me, he will obey my teaching. My Father will love him, and we will come to him and make our home with him. He who does not love me will not obey my teaching" (John 14:23–24).

What Jesus looks for in us is obedience generated by love rather than fear or self-interest. Without that motivation, our actions are something less than true obedience. As Paul wrote to the Corinthians, we can teach with power, master Scripture and even give all we possess to the poor, but if we "have not love," we gain nothing (1 Corinthians 13:1–3).

Love for Jesus is essential for one's own personal transformation. As long as believers are motivated by a desire to ensure salvation, Satan keeps us from becoming all God intends us to be. And this is a significant victory for evil over good in Satan's invisible war with God.

The second tactic is to intensify feelings of guilt. In thinking about guilt, we need to make a distinction between real guilt and guilt feelings. The first is objective: We bear the responsibility for any sin we commit, and thus *are* guilty. The second is subjective: Our consciences accuse us of having done wrong, and we *feel* guilty.

In Sunday school yesterday one of the class members shared her feelings of guilt and her frustration. She is a Christian now. But every day she is aware of a hundred little things she says or does that make her feel guilty. As a Christian she ought to be better than she is, and the guilt feelings torment her. What can she do?

I said I would tell her, but it would sound ridiculous. She nodded, so I said, "Stop taking yourself so seriously. When something you do makes you feel guilty, tell Jesus you've goofed again, and forget it. The sin is gone. Jesus paid for it on the cross."

Hebrews 10 takes up the issue of guilt and guilt feelings. The unidentified writer of this New Testament book looks back on Old Testament times and at the annual sacrifices that were "repeated endlessly year after year" (Hebrews 10:1). These sacrifices covered sins, but they could not take away sins. If they actually cleansed the worshipers, they "would no longer have felt guilty for their sins" (verse 4). Shifting focus to the cross, the writer reminds us that we have been made holy through the "once for all" sacrifice of Jesus on Calvary (verse 10). Now we can "draw near to God . . . in full assurance of faith," as the blood of Christ has cleansed us from a guilty conscience (verse 22).

Put simply, Jesus has dealt with our sins once and for all. We no longer are expected to bear their weight. Christ's blood has freed us from living with a guilty conscience.

Why, then, is Satan so invested in whispering reminders of sins in Christians' ears? Satan understands very well that guilt-driven actions can never produce the results God desires. Only love, not guilt, can produce disciples.

The third tactic is to intensify shame. Guilt feelings are usually associated with shame. Shame drives us to hide our true selves from each other. Satan is eager to intensify our sense of shame because he knows that a key to our growth as Christians is to experience Christ's unconditional love in a community of believers (see Ephesians 3:17–19).

Satan often tells us that if we are truly honest with each other we will somehow misrepresent Jesus and what He can do for believers. Satan knows, as the apostle Paul knew, this is a lie. In 2 Corinthians 3:12–18, Paul draws for us a contrast between Christians and Moses. Moses put a veil over his face to keep the Israelites from realizing the glow that marked his face after meeting with God was fading away. We, Paul explains, remove the veil, for it is with unveiled faces that we "reflect the Lord's glory." What others are to see is the Holy Spirit at work in our lives to transform us.

Others see the reality of Jesus in our lives not because we appear to be without fears or flaws. They see the reality of Jesus as we share ourselves and, over time, they see that we truly are "being transformed into [Jesus'] likeness with ever increasing glory" (2 Corinthians 3:18).

The more effective Satan is in focusing our attention on ourselves rather than Jesus, and intensifying our feelings of guilt and shame, the greater the victory of evil over good.

Overcoming Evil with Good

To be able to identify Satan's lies and to overcome his evil with good we need to understand what our salvation entails.

Salvation in the Old Testament

There are a number of Hebrew words related to the Old Testament view of salvation. The fascinating thing for us is that these terms are applied to specific, concrete situations that arise in our world. The New Testament view of salvation as personal deliverance from the power of sin and the devil is not found in the Old Testament, though there might be veiled references to this in Psalm 51:14; 79:9 and Ezekiel 37:23.

The model for developing the concept of salvation is the deliverance of the Israelites from slavery in Egypt. The Israelites were in a situation where they were helpless and could not free themselves. God chose a man, Moses, to be the agent through whom He would accomplish deliverance. And God unleashed His supernatural power to defeat the powers of darkness and free the Israelite slaves.

These elements are typically present where the Old Testament speaks of saving or salvation. An individual, group or, in this case, nation is in a desperate and helpless situation. God sends someone through whom He will bring deliverance, and exercises His supernatural power to provide freedom. In the Old Testament it is always God who acts to effect salvation. He accomplishes something that His people recognize they can never do.

Salvation in the New Testament

The core concept established in the Old Testament is carried over into the New. But here the concept is broadened. Rather than relate solely to concrete situations in this world, the New Testament broadens the focus to include the spiritual world. We human beings are seen as victims of our own sin and of Satan's control of human cultures. We are in bondage to sin, to death and to the devil. Only Jesus can free us from their grip.

The Greek words used in the New Testament are *sozo* ("to save") and its derivative, *soteria* ("salvation"). Many of the more than one hundred uses of these terms in the New Testament refer to deliverance from some physical threat (see Matthew 27:42; Acts 27:20, 31). And in passages referring to Jesus' miracles, *sozo* means "to restore to health and wholeness" (see Matthew 9:21–22; Luke 7:50). But in most contexts, *sozo* and *soteria* describe how God's action in Christ delivers us from the power of sin, death and Satan.

When extended to the spiritual, the same basic elements are found in the New Testament concept of salvation as in the Old. We humans are enslaved spiritually and cannot free ourselves. God sends a man, Jesus, to deliver us. To accomplish this deliverance God unleashes His supernatural power, raising Jesus from the dead.

What is the deliverance we have in Jesus today? We believers have complete forgiveness of sins, victory over the power of sin in our lives, and future resurrection to an eternity in God's community of love. As we read closely we see that these aspects are reflected in the use of the verb *to save*. "We were saved" (past) assures us of forgiveness of sin. "We are being saved" (present) invites us to rely on Jesus for power over sin in our lives today. "We will be saved" (future) promises resurrection to a new life in God's eternal community of love.

(1) *We were saved.* Paul, addressing two young disciples who would succeed him as leaders in the Christian movement, wrote, "He saved us . . . because of his mercy" (Titus 3:5), and "[God] has saved us and called us to a holy life" (2 Timothy 1:9). These and many other references in Scripture look back to the cross. Jesus was born into our world

as a baby, He lived a human life, and He was condemned to be crucified by Pontius Pilate, the Roman governor of Judea. Jesus did die on the cross. He was resurrected, and in His resurrection He was "declared with power to be the Son of God" (Romans 1:4). These are all things that happened in history—real history, not in myth or fantasy.

This anchor in history allows New Testament writers to affirm confidently that "Christ was sacrificed once to take away the sins of many people." When Scripture affirms that "he himself bore our sins in his body on the tree" (1 Peter 2:24), it directs our attention to Calvary, and reminds us that Christ has brought salvation to humankind. Because we believe that Christ died for us, we have been saved. All we can do is trust in His finished work. When we do trust, all Christ won for us is given to us, so we can say with confidence that we, personally, have been saved.

(2) *We are being saved.* Answers to our questions about all three aspects of salvation are developed in the book of Romans. Paul argues in the first three chapters that all have sinned and fallen short. In chapter 4, Paul draws attention to Abraham, and to the fact that even though he, too, fell short, God counted his faith as righteousness. God will credit us with righteousness as well if we trust Him as Abraham did.

In Romans 5 Paul reminds us that although death cast its shroud over humankind when Adam sinned, Christ, in His resurrection, brought us the gift of eternal life. Then in chapters 6 through 8 of Romans, Paul explores the impact of Christ's death on our present experience. In chapter 6 Paul expresses his frustration. He agrees with everything God says about what is right and good. But as hard as he tries, he keeps falling short and sinning. Sin has what seems to be an unbreakable grip on Paul.

Paul finds the answer to his quandary in the fact that God does more than consider us to have died with Christ: Our faith unites us to Jesus with a living, unbreakable bond. This means not only that our sins were paid for in His death, but also that the resurrection power flowing from Jesus is available to us, to free us from sin's grip on our lives now.

As with past-tense salvation, present-tense salvation is a trust issue. We are to "count" ourselves "dead to sin" and reject sinful impulses. But we cannot experience this freedom if we place ourselves "under law" (Romans 6:11, 14). That phrase means to try in our own strength to do what we know we ought to do.

Romans 8 provides God's solution. The flow of Jesus' resurrection power, channeled through the Holy Spirit, enables us to live righteous lives. This is living under grace rather than Law. Under grace we see Scripture as the Holy Spirit's prompting, and we respond not because we ought to, but because we love Jesus. Paul sums up this section with a word of triumph: "If the Spirit of him who raised Jesus from the dead is living in you, he who raised Christ from the dead will also give life to your mortal bodies through his Spirit, who lives in you" (Romans 8:11).

No wonder Satan wants us to doubt our salvation. If we cannot trust Jesus for forgiveness, how can we trust Him for the power to live righteous lives? Satan wants us to feel guilt and shame. The more guilt we feel, the harder we try to obey God. And the harder we try, the less we rely.

(3) *We will be saved.* As Paul moves on, he looks ahead. When Jesus comes again we will share in His glory. The creation will also be "liberated from its bondage to decay and brought into the glorious freedom of the children of God" (Romans 8:21).

Paul concludes with a great affirmation of faith:

> I am convinced that neither death nor life, neither angels nor demons, neither the present nor the future, nor any powers, neither height nor depth, nor anything else in all creation, will be able to separate us from the love of God that is in Christ Jesus our Lord.
>
> Romans 8:38–39

Learning to Trust Completely

1. Review the Bible passages quoted or referred to in this chapter. Meditate on each verse or passage. As you read, write down what stands out to you.

2. Read 1 John 1. John is writing about our experience of fellowship with God. Walking in light is a powerful image. When we walk in light we are being honest, not trying to deceive God or ourselves about anything we do. When we walk in light we are honest about our sins, and are invited to confess them. With confession, God removes any barrier in our relationship with Him, and continues to "purify us from all unrighteousness" (1 John 1:9).

   Confession of sins is linked here with our experience of God in our lives (fellowship). Not with salvation. We who have been saved maintain a close relationship with the Lord in part by confessing our sins, and trusting Him to forgive and cleanse.

   If confessing sins as soon as we become aware of them has not been your practice, begin that practice now.

3. Any time you feel uncertainty, guilt or shame remember Jesus' death and resurrection, and just give thanks.

16

The Gift of Unconditional Acceptance

We humans are spiritual beings. That is, God created us with an innate awareness that there is more to our existence than life in this world. We are aware that there is a world beyond our world, a world that impacts our lives and future. The apostle Paul even goes so far as to claim that "what may be known about God [from the creation] is plain to [humanity], because God has made it plain to them" (Romans 1:19). Paul explains that what may be known about God from the created universe is His "eternal power and divine nature" (verse 20). A personal God, with power far beyond ours, does exist.

There is nothing that Satan can do to eradicate this awareness from human consciousness. So Satan adopted a simple strategy. He would suppress humankind's knowledge of the true God and His love, and would offer humankind counterfeit gods. Satan has been successful at this. People in every culture acknowledge and worship some counterfeit deity. Here in the West those deities too often are money, fame and pleasure. Satan has a primary strategy he uses to keep First World people from establishing a personal relationship with Christ. Here in the West, Satan seeks to *suppress effective communication of the Gospel of God's redeeming love.*

Satan's first priority in the invisible war is keeping humans from knowing and loving God, and thus enjoying the eternal community of love He has provided.

Satan's Strategy Exposed

At the core of Christianity is a personal relationship with Jesus Christ. Believers' relationships with non-Christians are also vitally important. In the first century there were no radio or TV ministries spreading the Gospel over the airwaves. There were no Christian bookstores, no mega-churches. Christian faith was spread, not by mass media, but one to one, as believers shared the good news of God's love with friends, neighbors and co-workers.

This personal evangelism was effective. The Church father Tertullian (160–225) could rightly claim that in the Roman province of Africa, Christians were "all but a majority in every city!" The communication of the Gospel through most of the Christian era has relied almost entirely on sharing the love of Jesus one on one. Satan understands this completely, and has devised ways to suppress personal evangelism. Satan's strategy has two goals: to cause unbelievers to dismiss anything a Christian might say, and to intimidate believers into silence.

The first tactic is to establish dominant conflicting values. Today in America "tolerance" is firmly established as a dominant cultural value. Generally tolerance is a good thing, But Satan has so twisted this "good" until today tolerance is generally viewed as *the preeminent* value. If a believer expresses any of his convictions, he is accused of intolerance. Since most convictions that conflict with politically correct views are associated with Christianity, people feel justified in ignoring what "intolerant" believers may have to say about anything . . . and in feeling morally superior.

All too often, aware that others tend to view our beliefs as intolerant, we Christians hesitate to speak up and share the Gospel. Certainly the notion that Jesus is the only way to God is quickly dismissed in our culture as just another example of intolerance. A Christian who knows the truth, and who speaks up to affirm or defend it, is almost sure to be charged with a lack of tolerance.

Satan has succeeded in refashioning something that generally *is* good—tolerance—into a tool of evil, which he uses to suppress expression of what is truly good.

The second tactic is to apply deceptive labels. Satan is an expert at renaming evil. Thus, sexually explicit material is not called "pornographic," but rather "adult." Abortion is framed as an issue of a woman's right to choose what to do with her own body. The use of *right* and *choose*, with the phrase *her own body*, distorts the issue. The fact is that an unborn child is a completely different person from the woman who is carrying him or her. The fetus has his or her own individual genetic stamp, and will emerge at birth as a unique person.

One way Christians and others attempt to counter this tactic of Satan is to reframe the issue. Thus the "pro-choice" movement (which gives the appearance of something good although rooted in a lie) has led to the development of a "pro-life" movement, rooted in reality and affirming the value and worth of every human being, born or unborn.

Even so, Satan's use of deceptive labels has proven effective. Those who accept and use his terminology uncritically also claim the moral high ground, and once again find reason not to listen to those looking to Scripture for light on those points.

The third tactic is to utilize social pressure. The desire to belong is deeply embedded in most human beings. We want to fit in and to be accepted by others. But there is a price to pay for acceptance, and that price typically is conformity. To be accepted by others we must strive to be, or at least appear to be, like them.

There are, of course, limits to what we will do to be accepted. When we resist the most obvious evils others practice we may find ourselves in the situation described in 1 Peter 4:4: "They think it strange that you do not plunge with them into the same flood of dissipation, and they heap abuse on you."

Typically, though, the pressure to fit in is far subtler. We are expected to chat over lunch about how our sports team is doing, to hear "the latest" on a co-worker's disastrous romances or to talk about the TV program everyone saw last night. We are expected to stick to the superficial. Probing into hurts or failures is out of bounds, just as bringing up controversial subjects like religion or politics is frowned upon. Satan's watchword, "Go along to get along," rules. As long as we keep on the surface of life and act in a friendly way, we are accepted as one of the group.

Subtle social pressure to conform is one of the tactics Satan uses to suppress communication of the Gospel. To offer prayer, to ask about a person's relationship with God, to talk about the love of Jesus is not what others want. And when we do not conform, we sense a loss of acceptance. We *feel* that we do not belong, and a sense of belonging is so important most are unwilling to risk its loss.

The fourth tactic Satan uses to suppress communication of the Gospel is fear of failure. Satan whispers, "You don't know enough. What if someone asks a question you can't answer? If you speak up, you'll be rejected and ridiculed. Or, your answer will turn the person off on Christianity forever!"

Nearly all Christians feel they do not know enough to be able to deal with questions or objections others might raise. So we rationalize, telling ourselves that because we do not know enough, we could do more harm than good. We hold back . . . and Satan's effort to suppress communication of the Gospel has won.

Satan's tactics have proven very effective against the kind of one-on-one sharing of the Gospel that marked its communication in the first century. By establishing dominant cultural values, by deceptive labeling, by utilizing social pressure and by encouraging fear of failure, Satan has marginalized Christians in the eyes of society. And he has held Christians back from the kind of witness that so impacted the first-century world.

Overcoming Evil with Good

Most Christians are blind to the fact that there is a truly simple way to counter the evil embedded in Satan's tactics, and to overcome this evil with good.

We were surprised when Charlie and Barbara, a couple none of us had met, showed up at the small group I led. At that time we were members of a Wesleyan Methodist church in Scottsdale, Arizona. A few years before, the pastor, Bob Girard, had founded what all too quickly became a "typical" church, focused on providing programs for children, young people and adults. Then Bob read some magazine articles I had written exploring a biblical vision of the Church. Bob became convinced that "typical" churches did not fit God's vision for local bodies of believers.

A year or so after Bob had read the articles, I moved to Phoenix and became personally involved in the church he led. While the Scottsdale church still provided classes for children and youth, the focus had shifted to the nurturing of adults. Within a few years some 80 percent of adults in the church met weekly in what we called CHUM (Christian Home Unit Meeting) gatherings. It was primarily through these small house groups that each year we saw about as many reached for Christ as we had members. Usually this happened simply by CHUM group members inviting someone to join them.

It was a little different with Charlie and Barbara. They happened to visit our Sunday service on a day I was preaching, and decided they wanted to visit the group I led.

We were delighted to welcome them. Charlie was quiet, a successful developer, and his wife, Barbara, a delightful, outgoing individual. Our group process was simple. We looked at a passage of Scripture and each shared what God was saying to him or her through it. We talked about what was happening in each of our lives. And we prayed for each other. Though the process was simple, it was clear that here was a group of people who loved each other, who cared deeply about one another's trials and joys.

This was all new to Charlie and Barbara, even though they had been brought up in church, and were currently attending a church in their neighborhood. At first they were quiet, but as the weeks passed and they became more comfortable, they began to share and to ask questions. It was several months later that Barbara apologized, saying that she and Charlie had only recently come to know Jesus as their Savior.

"We really felt bad," she explained. "All those weeks we were coming, and you thought we were real Christians."

I had to laugh. "Barbara," I told her, "we knew you weren't 'real Christians' all along. But it didn't make any difference. We loved you anyway."

My reaction seemed hard for Barbara to process. So I asked her, "Barbara, what would you have done if we'd made it clear we knew you weren't 'real Christians'? And that you had to believe what we believe in order to be welcome?"

She answered quickly. "We'd never have come back."

A few months after that, Barbara came to the group with a problem. Her mother lived in St. Louis, and was a member of the church Barb had grown up in. But Barbara was very aware that her mom did not know Jesus in the personal way that Barbara now experienced Him. So Barbara had begun earnestly telling her about Jesus and urging her to become a Christian, too. She had also been sending her mother Christian books. But now Barbara was frustrated. Each time Barbara sent a book, her mother would send some book in return.

"What can I do?" Barbara asked, upset and deeply concerned for her mother. "It's getting to the point where we can't talk with each other anymore."

I asked Barbara to recall the conversation we had had when she and Charlie told us they had each come to know Jesus as Savior. I asked her again, "What would you have done if we'd made it clear we knew you weren't 'real Christians'?"

She gave the same answer. "We'd never have come back."

"Barbara," I explained, "we don't bring people to Jesus by letting them know they're different from us, or by implying that to be accepted they have to believe what we believe. We bring people to Jesus simply by loving them as they are, and inviting them into our lives so they can see who Jesus is to us.

"All you need to do," I went on, "is to treat your mother as if she's already a 'real Christian.' Love her where and as she is. Tell your mom what's going on with you and Charlie. Talk about what Jesus is doing in your life, just as you talk so naturally about Him here with us."

With great relief Barbara said, "I can't wait to talk to my mom tomorrow."

This experience with Charlie and Barbara illustrates the power of unconditional acceptance. Simply put, unconditional acceptance is a commitment to love and welcome others, whoever they are and whatever they believe. Unconditional acceptance extends an invitation to others to become a part of our lives, and expresses willingness to become part of theirs. Unconditional acceptance means that we do not charge the price of conformity—agreement with our beliefs or with our values—to those we welcome into our lives. In short, unconditional acceptance creates a relational context in which the Gospel can be shared effectively.

Unconditional acceptance is not magical, nor does it guarantee quick conversion. Radical acceptance is simply revealing, in our relationship with others, the nature of God's love relationship with us. And we continue to do this even if the response is not what we hope it will be.

José was a fighter pilot at the nearby air force base when he and his wife, Laura, joined our group. José had recently come to know Christ, and had committed himself completely to the Lord. Laura was not a believer, and was deeply disturbed by her husband's suddenly strange behavior. A few months later, Laura asked José to move out of their home.

As I talked with her it became clear that she had experienced in our group the same unconditional acceptance that Barbara and Charlie had, even though she had made it clear to the group immediately that she was not a believer. She said that she recognized and valued our love, but what she called her husband's strange behavior was too much for her.

It is here we see how Satan again enters the picture. Paul writes that "the god of this age" has "blinded the minds of unbelievers so that they cannot see the light of the gospel" (2 Corinthians 4:4). With Laura, our love and acceptance could not break through.

It is no wonder that Christians flounder when they try to explain the Gospel. In the marketplace of ideas we find ourselves accused of intolerance. Satan's relabeling of our values suggests that they are evil rather than good. Our stumbling efforts to explain what we believe often fall on deaf ears. But even the apostle Paul, educated in all the arguments of pagan philosophers and trained in the Scriptures by the Pharisees, chose not to rely on "eloquence or superior wisdom." Instead Paul resolved "to know nothing while I was with you except Jesus Christ and him crucified" (1 Corinthians 2:1–2). Jesus, and a personal relationship with Him, was Paul's focus. Even in Corinth, where great emphasis was put on "wisdom," Paul chose to rely completely on the simple message of God's love expressed in the crucified and risen Christ.

What is so fascinating is that while Satan's tactics are generally successful in misrepresenting Christians and Christianity, *none of his tactics is effective against sharing the Gospel in a context created by unconditional acceptance and love.*

Jesus came into our world, not to count our sins or hold them against us (see 2 Corinthians 5:19), but to invite us into a personal relationship with God. We are called to invite others to experience this kind of relationship with us. It is most often in the context of an accepting, welcoming relationship that others will meet, and be drawn to, Jesus Christ.

Love in All

The role of unconditional acceptance and love is woven throughout our discussions of overcoming Satan's evil with good. Its role within God's family is deeply embedded in pictures of the core community, of the family as a community of love, in God's design of Israel's society, in the church called to community and in the other of God's gifts that we have explored. In each setting, a context of unconditional love and acceptance is implied—and is crucial if we are going to war against Satan successfully by overcoming his evil with good.

In whatever situation where we interact with others, love and unconditional acceptance open the door to the experience of God's love in Jesus, and to our present experience of aspects of God's eternal community of love.

By practicing unconditional acceptance of others, we avoid the traps Satan has set to keep us from experiencing all that God has for us in Christ.

Expressing Unconditional Acceptance

1. Unconditional acceptance of a person does not require agreeing with sinful behavior.

2. Unconditional acceptance calls for us to love others who might have different values and beliefs.

3. Unconditional acceptance is an expression of Christ's love that others can experience.

4. An atmosphere of unconditional acceptance creates opportunities to witness.

5. Unconditional acceptance does not limit us from speaking the truth in love.

6. Treat and speak to others as though they are "real Christians."

7. Share freely what you *do* know of Jesus, without worrying about what you *do not* know.

8. The Holy Spirit convicts others of sin. We are to show others that Jesus loves them.

Epilogue

A Look Back

When God created human beings in His image and likeness, He had a truly wonderful purpose in mind. Just as the Father, Son and Holy Spirit lived in an intimate, perfect relationship of love, so God would create persons He could draw to Himself and who, ultimately, would share in an eternal community of love. So that love might be freely given, God created human beings with freedom of choice. In what seems at times to be a corruption of God's purpose, the first humans rather than bonding to the Lord chose independence. As Genesis 3 makes clear, they were encouraged to make the choice of independence by Satan, a rebel angel who had himself been given the gift of choice in the eons before what we call the Creation story of Genesis 1.

The great rebellion, led by Satan and the angels who chose to follow him, ended in disaster for the rebels. In descriptions of the great battle found in the prophets, described by Jesus and reviewed in Revelation, Satan and his followers were "thrown to earth," a ruined battlefield described in Genesis 1:1 as "formless and empty."

Then God acted to refashion the face of our planet and the universe itself, as described in the seven days of Genesis 1. And there God settled the first humans, to live as His representatives and to build on the good things He had fashioned.

This beachhead God established on earth by the creation of humans in His own image was too much for Satan. He determined to thwart God's purposes by alienating us from our original relationship with the Creator. And he succeeded—partially.

The Bible's story is essentially a story of the love of a God who refuses to give up on His creations. That love ultimately moved God to sacrifice Jesus, God the Son, to redeem us and free us from the deadly grip Satan had established on our race. As we are forgiven and adopted into God's family through faith in Jesus, God will yet bring us into that eternal community of love that awaits us.

A Look Ahead

But it was not enough for God to provide a community of love at history's end. God intended, and intends, for us to experience something of that community as we live our lives here on earth. To that end He has provided good gifts for His people, gifts through which we can experience His presence and build a bond of love with others.

Again, this has been more than Satan can bear. He has renewed his commitment to thwart God's purposes, this time by overcoming the good in God's gifts with evil. He has developed many strategies and tactics to twist, distort and corrupt the good gifts with evil . . . strategies and tactics we have looked at in this book.

But we, as Paul writes in Romans 12:21, are called to overcome evil with good. We are called to see ourselves as warriors in an invisible war between God and Satan, good and evil, that has raged for eons. As we recognize the strategies and tactics Satan uses to corrupt each good gift, we are able to follow the guidelines provided in God's Word and to overcome Satan's evil with good.

In a very real sense, while spiritual warfare sometimes pits individuals against demons who oppress them, and calls for us to use the authority Jesus gives us to cast the evil spirits out, the epic battle is being fought daily by believers who are committed to live by God's Word, and so confront Satan on a larger stage. As we do so, not only will we be taking part in tearing down the kingdom of evil Satan has established here on earth, we will also be given a taste of what the eternal Kingdom of love will be like.

So what lies ahead? What lies ahead, for you and for me and for all followers of Jesus, is the promise of victory as we step up to take our places in the ranks of God's spiritual warriors. And with that challenge we have the promise of a new, fresh and very real experience of the presence of God in our lives.

Index

Larry Richards holds a B.A. in philosophy from the University of Michigan, a Th.M. in Christian education from Dallas Theological Seminary, and a Ph.D. in religious education and social psychology from Garrett Biblical Seminary and Northwestern University jointly. He has taught in the Wheaton College Graduate School, served as a minister of Christian education, and written more than two hundred books, including theological works, commentaries, and several specialty and study Bibles. Larry is currently a full-time author and speaker. He and his wife, Sue, live in Raleigh, North Carolina.

More from Larry Richards

Stand firm against the devil's schemes with this ironclad, hands-on defense plan straight from the Bible. Using Paul's letter to the Ephesians as his guide, Richards reveals how God provides protection from every attack of the enemy—and how you can put on the full armor of God today.

The Full Armor of God

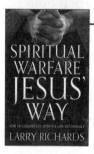

In this practical handbook, Richards offers a balanced, biblical approach to spiritual warfare using Jesus as a model. Drawing directly from Jesus' words and actions in the gospels, he explains how to recognize the enemy's tactics, prepare to face the enemy and help others who are under attack.

Spiritual Warfare Jesus' Way

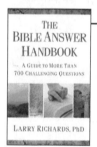

Find biblical answers to over 700 questions about the Bible! Working through the Bible book by book, Richards looks at a variety of perplexing questions on topics ranging from authorship and internal contradictions to historical inaccuracy. He also sheds light on the meaning of difficult passages, while always maintaining the view that the Bible is reliable and trustworthy.

The Bible Answer Handbook

✓Chosen

 Stay up-to-date on your favorite books and authors with our free e-newsletters. Sign up today at chosenbooks.com.

 Find us on Facebook. facebook.com/chosenbooks

 Follow us on Twitter. @Chosen_Books